CRACKNELL'S STATUTES

Succession

Second Edition

Edited by

D G Cracknell LLB
of the Middle Temple, Barrister

Series Editor

D G Cracknell LLB
of the Middle Temple, Barrister

Old Bailey Press

OLD BAILEY PRESS LIMITED
The Gatehouse, Ruck Lane, Horsmonden, Kent TN12 8EA

First published 1994
Second edition 1995

© Old Bailey Press Ltd 1995

ISBN 1 85836 043 9

British Library Cataloguing-in-Publication.

A CIP Catalogue record for this book is available from the
British Library.

Printed and bound in Great Britain.

CONTENTS

Contents

PREFACE

This book sets out, in their amended form, in whole or in part, the provisions of thirty-one statutes to which students will need to refer as they prepare for their Succession examination.

Of course, the relevant sections of the Wills Act 1837, the Administration of Estates Act 1925 and the Inheritance (Provision for Family and Dependants) Act 1975 are included, but all of the other provisions have an important bearing on particular aspects of the whole subject.

Amendments or substitutions made on or before 1 December 1994 have been taken into account and a note at the end of the particular statute indicates the source of any changes.

ALPHABETICAL TABLE OF STATUTES

STAMP ACT 1815
(35 Geo 3 c 184)

37 Penalty for administering effects of a deceased person without proving the will or taking out letters of administration within a given time

If any person shall take possession of and in any manner administer any part of the estate and effects of any person deceased without obtaining probate of the will or letters of administration of the estate and effects of the deceased within six calendar months after his or her decease or within two calendar months after the termination of any suit or dispute respecting the will or the right to letters of administration, if there shall be any such which shall not be ended within four calendar months after the death of the deceased, every person so offending shall forfeit the sum of one hundred pounds.

As amended by the Statute Law Revision (No 2) Act 1890; Finance Act 1975, ss52(2), (3), 59(5), Schedule 13, Pt I.

WILLS ACT 1837
(7 Will 4 & 1 Vict c 26)

1 Meaning of certain words in this Act

The words and expressions hereinafter mentioned, which in their ordinary signification have a more confined or a different meaning, shall in this Act, except where the nature of the provision or the context of the Act shall exclude such construction, be interpreted as follows: (that is to say,) the word 'will' shall extend to a testament, and to a codicil, and to an appointment by will or by writing in the nature of a will in exercise of a power, and also to an appointment by will of a guardian of a child, and to any other testamentary disposition; and the words 'real estate' shall extend to manors, advowsons, messuages, lands, tithes, rents, and hereditaments, whether freehold, customary freehold, tenant right, customary or copyhold, or of any other tenure, and whether corporeal, incorporeal, or personal, and to any undivided share thereof, and to any estate, right, or interest (other than a chattel interest) therein; and the words 'personal estate' shall extend to leasehold estates, and other chattels real, and also to moneys, shares of government and other funds, securities for money (being not real estates), debts, choses in action, rights, credits, goods, and all other property whatsoever, which by law devolves upon the executor or administrator, and to any share or interest therein; and every word importing the singular number only shall extend and be applied to several persons or things as well as one person or thing; and every word importing the masculine gender only shall extend and be applied to a female as well as a male.

3 All property may be disposed of by will

It shall be lawful for every person to devise, bequeath, or dispose of, by his will executed in manner hereinafter required, all real estate and all personal estate which he shall be entitled to, either at law or in equity, at the time of his death, and which, if not so devised, bequeathed, and disposed of, would devolve upon his executor or administrator; and the power hereby given shall extend to all contingent, executory or other future interests in any real or personal estate, whether the testator may or may not be ascertained as the person or one of the persons in whom the same respectively may become vested, and whether he may be entitled thereto under the instrument by which the same respectively were created, or under any disposition thereof by deed or will; and also to all rights of entry for conditions broken, and other rights of entry; and also to such of the same estates, interests, and rights respectively, and other real and personal estate, as the testator may be entitled to at the time of his death, notwithstanding that he may become entitled to the same subsequently to the execution of his will.

7   No will of a person under age valid

No will made by any person under the age of eighteen years shall be valid.

9   Signing and attestation of wills

No will shall be valid unless –

(a) it is in writing, and signed by the testator, or by some other person in his presence and by his direction; and

(b) it appears that the testator intended by his signature to give effect to the will; and

(c) the signature is made or acknowledged by the testator in the presence of two or more witnesses present at the same time; and

(d) each witness either –

(i) attests and signs the will; or

(ii) acknowledges his signature,

in the presence of the testator (but not necessarily in the presence of any other witness),

but no form of attestation shall be necessary.

10 Appointments by will to be executed like other wills, and to be valid, although other required solemnities are not observed

No appointment made by will, in exercise of any power, shall be valid, unless the same be executed in manner hereinbefore required; and every will executed in manner hereinbefore required shall, so far as respects the execution and attestation thereof, be a valid execution of a power of appointment by will, notwithstanding it shall have been expressly required that a will made in exercise of such power should be executed with some additional or other form of execution or solemnity.

11 Soldiers' and mariners' wills excepted

Provided always, that any soldier being in actual military service, or any mariner or seaman being at sea, may dispose of his personal estate as he might have done before the making of this Act.

13 Publication not to be requisite

Every will executed in manner hereinbefore required shall be valid without any other publication thereof.

14 Will not to be void on account of incompetency of attesting witness

If any person who shall attest the execution of a will shall at the time of the execution thereof or at any time afterwards be incompetent to be admitted a witness to prove the execution thereof, such will shall not on that account be invalid.

15 Gifts to an attesting witness to be void

If any person shall attest the execution of any will to whom or to whose wife or husband any beneficial devise, legacy, estate, interest, gift, or appointment, of or affecting any real or personal estate (other than and except charges and directions for the payment of any debt or debts), shall be thereby given or made, such devise, legacy, estate, gift, or appointment shall, so far only as concerns such person attesting the execution of such will, or the wife or husband of such person, or any person claiming under such person or wife, or husband, be utterly null and void, and such person so attesting shall be admitted as a witness to prove the execution of such will, or to prove the validity or invalidity thereof, notwithstanding such devise, legacy, estate, interest, gift, or appointment mentioned in such will.

16 Creditor attesting to be admitted a witness

In case by any will any real or personal estate shall be charged with any debt or debts, and any creditor, or the wife or husband of any creditor, whose debt is so charged, shall attest the execution of such will, such creditor notwithstanding such charge shall be admitted a witness to prove the execution of such will, or to prove the validity or invalidity thereof.

17 Executor to be admitted a witness

No person shall, on account of his being an executor of a will, be incompetent to be admitted a witness to prove the execution of such will, or a witness to prove the validity or invalidity thereof.

18 Will to be revoked by marriage

(1) Subject to subsections (2) to (4) below, a will shall be revoked by the testator's marriage.

(2) A disposition in a will in exercise of a power of appointment shall take effect notwithstanding the testator's subsequent marriage unless the property so appointed would in default of appointment pass to his personal representatives.

(3) Where it appears from a will that at the time it was made the testator was expecting to be married to a particular person and that he intended that the will should not be revoked by the marriage, the will shall not be revoked by his marriage to that person.

(4) Where it appears from a will that at the time it was made the testator was expecting to be married to a particular person and that he intended that a disposition in the will should not be revoked by his marriage to that person –

　　(a) that disposition shall take effect notwithstanding the marriage; and

(b) any other disposition in the will shall take effect also, unless it appears from the will that the testator intended the disposition to be revoked by the marriage.

18A Effect of dissolution or annulment of marriage on wills

(1) Where, after a testator has made a will, a decree of a court of civil jurisdiction in England and Wales dissolves or annuls his marriage or his marriage is dissolved or annulled and the divorce or annulment is entitled to recognition in England and Wales by virtue of Part II of the Family Law Act 1986, –

(a) the will shall take effect as if any appointment of the former spouse as an executor or as the executor and trustee of the will were omitted; and

(b) any devise or bequest to the former spouse shall lapse,

except in so far as a contrary intention appears by the will.

(2) Subsection (1)(b) above is without prejudice to any right of the former spouse to apply for financial provision under the Inheritance (Provision for Family and Dependants) Act 1975.

(3) Where –

(a) by the terms of a will an interest in remainder is subject to a life interest; and

(b) the life interest lapses by virtue of subsection (1)(b) above,

the interest in remainder shall be treated as if it had not been subject to the life interest and, if it was contingent upon the termination of the life interest, as if it had not been so contingent.

19 No will to be revoked by presumption

No will shall be revoked by any presumption of an intention on the ground of an alteration in circumstances.

20 No will to be revoked otherwise than by another will or codicil, or by a writing executed like a will, or by destruction

No will or codicil, or any part thereof, shall be revoked otherwise than as aforesaid, or by another will or codicil executed in manner hereinbefore required, or by some writing declaring an intention to revoke the same, and executed in the manner in which a will is hereinbefore required to be executed, or by the burning, tearing, or otherwise destroying the same by the testator, or by some person in his presence and by his direction, with the intention of revoking the same.

21 No alteration in a will shall have any effect unless executed as a will

No obliteration, interlineation, or other alteration made in any will after the execution thereof shall be valid or have any effect, except so far as the words or effect of the will before such alteration shall not be apparent, unless such alteration shall be executed in like manner as hereinbefore is required for the execution of the will; but the will, with such alteration as part thereof, shall be deemed to be duly executed if the signature of the testator and the subscription of the witnesses be made in the margin or on some other part of the will opposite or near to such alteration, or at the foot or end of or opposite to a memorandum referring to such alteration, and written at the end or some other part of the will.

22 No will revoked to be revived otherwise than by re-execution or a codicil to revive it

No will or codicil, or any part thereof, which shall be in any manner revoked, shall be revived otherwise than by the re-execution thereof, or by a codicil executed in manner hereinbefore required, and showing an intention to revive the same; and when any will or codicil which shall be partly revoked, and afterwards wholly revoked, shall be revived, such revival shall not extend to so much thereof as shall have been revoked before the revocation of the whole thereof, unless an intention to the contrary shall be shown.

23 A devise not to be rendered inoperative by any subsequent conveyance or act

No conveyance or other act made or done subsequently to the execution of a will of or relating to any real or personal estate therein comprised, except an act by which such will shall be revoked as aforesaid, shall prevent the operation of the will with respect to such estate or interest in such real or personal estate as the testator shall have power to dispose of by will at the time of his death.

24   A will shall be construed to speak from the death of the testator

Every will shall be construed, with reference to the real estate and personal estate comprised in it, to speak and take effect as if it had been executed immediately before the death of the testator, unless a contrary intention shall appear by the will.

25   A residuary devise shall include estates comprised in lapsed and void devises

Unless a contrary intention shall appear by the will, such real estate or interest therein as shall be comprised or intended to be comprised in any devise in such will contained, which shall fail or be void by reason of the death of the devisee in the lifetime of the testator, or by reason of such devise being contrary to law or otherwise incapable of taking effect, shall be included in the residuary devise (if any) contained in such will.

26   A general devise of the testator's lands shall include leasehold as well as freehold lands

A devise of the land of the testator, or of the land of the testator in any place or in the occupation of any person mentioned in his will, or otherwise described in a general manner, and any other general devise which would describe a leasehold estate if the testator had no freehold estate which could be described by it, shall be construed to include the leasehold estates of the testator, or any of them, to which such description shall extend, as the case may be, as well as freehold estates, unless a contrary intention shall appear by the will.

27   A general gift shall include estates over which the testator has a general power of appointment

A general devise of the real estate of the testator, or of the real estate of the testator in any place or in the occupation of any person mentioned in his will, or otherwise described in a general manner, shall be construed to include any real estate, or any real estate to which such description shall extend (as the case may be), which he may have power to appoint in any manner he may think proper, and shall operate as an execution of such power, unless a contrary intention shall appear by the will; and in like manner a bequest of the personal estate of the testator, or any bequest of personal property described in a general manner, shall be construed to include any personal estate, or any personal estate to which such description shall extend (as the case may be), which he may have power to appoint in any manner he may think proper, and shall operate as an execution of such power, unless a contrary intention shall appear by the will.

28 A devise without any words of limitation shall be construed to pass the fee

Where any real estate shall be devised to any person without any words of limitation, such devise shall be construed to pass the fee simple, or other the whole estate or interest which the testator had power to dispose of by will in such real estate, unless a contrary intention shall appear by the will.

29 The words 'die without issue', or 'die without leaving issue', shall be construed to mean die without issue living at the death

In any devise or bequest of real or personal estate the words 'die without issue' or 'die without leaving issue', or 'have no issue', or any other words which may import either a want or failure of issue of any person in his lifetime or at the time of his death, or an indefinite failure of his issue, shall be construed to mean a want or failure of issue in the lifetime or at the time of the death of such person, and not an indefinite failure of his issue, unless a contrary intention shall appear by the will, by reason of such person having a prior estate tail, or of a preceding gift, being, without any implication arising from such words, a limitation of an estate tail to such person or issue, or otherwise: Provided, that this Act shall not extend to cases where such words as aforesaid import if no issue described in a preceding gift shall be born, or if there shall be no issue who shall live to attain the age or otherwise answer the description required for obtaining a vested estate by a preceding gift to such issue.

32 Devises of estates tail shall not lapse

Where any person to whom any real estate shall be devised for an estate tail or an estate in quasi entail shall die in the lifetime of the testator leaving issue who would be inheritable under such entail, and any such issue shall be living at the time of the death of the testator, such devise shall not lapse, but shall take effect as if the death of such person had happened immediately after the death of the testator, unless a contrary intention shall appear by the will.

33 Gifts to children or other issue who leave issue living at the testator's death shall not lapse

(1) Where –

(a) a will contains a devise or bequest to a child or remoter descendant of the testator; and

(b) the intended beneficiary dies before the testator, leaving issue; and

(c) issue of the intended beneficiary are living at the testator's death,

then, unless a contrary intention appears by the will, the devise or bequest shall take effect as a devise or bequest to the issue living at the testator's death.

(2) Where –

(a) a will contains a devise or bequest to a class of person consisting of children or remoter descendants of the testator; and

(b) a member of the class dies before the testator, leaving issue, and

(c) issue of that member are living at the testator's death,

then, unless a contrary intention appears by the will, the devise or bequest shall take effect as if the class included the issue of its deceased member living at the testator's death.

(3) Issue shall take under this section through all degrees, according to their stock, in equal shares if more than one, any gift or share which their parent would have taken and so that no issue shall take whose parent is living at the testator's death and that no issue shall take whose parent is living at the testator's death and so capable of taking.

(4) For the purposes of this section –

(a) the illegitimacy of any person is to be disregarded; and

(b) a person conceived before the testator's death and born living thereafter is to be taken to have been living at the testator's death.

34 Act not to extend to wills made before 1838, or to estates pur autre vie of persons who die before 1838

This Act shall not extend to any will made before the first day of January one thousand eight hundred and thirty-eight, and every will re-executed or republished, or revived by any codicil, shall for the purposes of this Act be deemed to have been made at the time at which the same shall be so re-executed, republished, or revived; and this Act shall not extend to any estate pur autre vie of any person who shall die before the first day of January one thousand eight hundred and thirty-eight.

As amended by the Statute Law Revision (No 2) Act 1888; Statute Law Revision Act 1893; Statute Law (Repeals) Act 1969; Family Law Reform Act 1969, s3(1)(a); Administration of Justice Act 1982, ss17, 18(1), (2), 19; Family Law Act 1986, s53; Children Act 1989, s108(5), Schedule 13, para 1.

APPORTIONMENT ACT 1870
(33 & 34 Vict c 35)

2   Rents, etc to be apportionable in respect of time

All rents, annuities, dividends, and other periodical payments in the nature of income (whether reserved or made payable under an instrument in writing or otherwise) shall, like interest on money lent, be considered as accruing from day to day, and shall be apportionable in respect of time accordingly.

3   Apportioned part of rent, etc to be payable when the next entire portion shall have become due

The apportioned part of any such rent, annuity, dividend, or other payment shall be payable or recoverable in the case of a continuing rent, annuity, or other such payment when the entire portion of which such apportioned part shall form part shall become due and payable, and not before, and in the case of a rent, annuity, or other such payment determined by re-entry, death, or otherwise when the next entire portion of the same would have been payable if the same had not so determined, and not before.

7   Nor where stipulation made to the contrary

The provisions of this Act shall not extend to any case in which it is or shall be expressly stipulated that no apportionment shall take place.

As amended by the Statute Law Revision (No 2) Act 1893.

REVENUE ACT 1884
(47 & 48 Vict c 62)

11 Representation in the United Kingdom to constitute the title to assets therein situate

Notwithstanding any provision to the contrary contained in any local or private Act of Parliament, the production of a grant of representation from a court in the United Kingdom by probate or letters of administration or confirmation shall be necessary to establish the right to recover or receive any part of the personal estate and effects of any deceased person situated in the United Kingdom. Provided that where a policy of life assurance has been effected with any insurance company by a person who shall die domiciled elsewhere than in the United Kingdom, the production of a grant of representation from a court in the United Kingdom shall not be necessary to establish the right to receive the money payable in respect of such policy.

As amended by the Revenue Act 1889, s19.

PARTNERSHIP ACT 1890
(53 & 54 Vict c 39)

2 Rules for determining existence of partnership

In determining whether a partnership does or does not exist, regard shall be had to the following rules: ...

(3) The receipt by a person of a share of the profits of a business is prima facie evidence that he is a partner in the business, but receipt of such a share, or of a payment contingent on or varying with the profits of a business, does not of itself make him a partner in the business; and in particular ...

(d) The advance of money by way of loan to a person engaged or about to engage in any business on a contract with that person that the lender shall receive a rate of interest varying with the profits, or shall receive a share of the profits arising from carrying on the business, does not of itself make the lender a partner with the person or persons carrying on the business or liable as such. Provided that the contract is in writing, and signed by or on behalf of all the parties thereto: ...

3 Postponement of rights of person lending or selling in consideration of share of profits in case of insolvency

In the event of any person to whom money has been advanced by way of loan upon such a contract as is mentioned in the last foregoing section, or of any buyer of a goodwill in consideration of a share of the profits of the business, being adjudged a bankrupt, entering into an arrangement to pay his creditors less than 100p in the pound, or dying in insolvent circumstances, the lender of the loan shall not be entitled to recover anything in respect of his loan, and the seller of the goodwill shall not be entitled to recover anything in respect of the share of profits contracted for, until the claims of the other creditors of the borrower or buyer for valuable consideration in money or money's worth have been satisfied.

As amended by the Decimal Currency Act 1969, s10(1).

WILLS (SOLDIERS AND SAILORS) ACT 1918
(7 & 8 Geo 5 c 58)

1 Explanation of s11 of Wills Act 1837

In order to remove doubts as to the construction of the Wills Act 1837, it is hereby declared and enacted that section 11 of that Act authorises and always has authorised any soldier being in actual military service, or any mariner or seaman being at sea, to dispose of his personal estate as he might have done before the passing of that Act, though under the age of eighteen years.

2 Extension of s11 of the Wills Act 1837

Section 11 of the Wills Act 1837 shall extend to any member of His Majesty's naval or marine forces not only when he is at sea but also when he is so circumstanced that if he were a soldier he would be in actual military service within the meaning of that section.

3 Validity of testamentary dispositions of real property made by soldiers and sailors

(1) A testamentary disposition of any real estate in England or Ireland made by a person to whom section 11 of the Wills Act 1837, applies, and who dies after the passing of this Act, shall, notwithstanding that the person making the disposition was at the time of making it under eighteen years of age or that the disposition has not been made in such manner or form as was at the passing of this Act required by law, be valid in any case where the person making the disposition was of such age and the disposition has been made in such manner and form that if the disposition had been a disposition of personal estate made by such a person domiciled in England or Ireland it would have been valid.

4   Power to appoint testamentary guardians

Where any person dies after the passing of this Act having made a will which is, or which, if it had been a disposition of property, would have been rendered valid by s11 of the Wills Act 1837, any appointment contained in that will of any person as guardian of the infant children of the testator shall be of full force and effect.

5   Short title and interpretation

(2) For the purposes of section 11 of the Wills Act 1837 and this Act the expression 'soldier' includes a member of the Air Force, and references in this Act to the said section 11 include a reference to that section as explained and extended by this Act.

As amended by the Family Law Reform Act 1969, s3(1)(b).

TRUSTEE ACT 1925
(15 & 16 Geo 5 c 19)

14 Power of trustees to give receipts

(1) The receipt in writing of a trustee for any money, securities, or other personal property or effects payable, transferable, or deliverable to him under any trust or power shall be a sufficient discharge to the person paying, transferring, or delivering the same and shall effectual exonerate him from seeing to the application or being answerable for any loss or misapplication thereof.

(2) This section does not, except where the trustee is a trust corporation, enable a sole trustee to give a valid receipt for –

　(a) the proceeds of sale or other capital money arising under a trust for sale of land;

　(b) capital money arising under the Settled Land Act 1925.

(3) This section applies notwithstanding anything to the contrary in the instrument, if any, creating the trust.

15 Power to compound liabilities

A personal representative, or two or more trustees acting together, or, subject to the restrictions imposed in regard to receipts by a sole trustee not being a trust corporation, a sole acting trustee where by the instrument, if any, creating the trust, or by statute, a sole trustee is authorised to execute the trusts and powers reposed in him, may, if and as he or they think fit –

　(a) accept any property, real or personal, before the time at which it is made transferable or payable; or

　(b) sever and apportion any blended trust funds or property; or

　(c) pay or allow any debt or claim on any evidence that he or they think sufficient; or

(d) accept any composition or any security, real or personal, for any debt or for any property, real or personal, claimed; or

(e) allow any time for payment of any debt; or

(f) compromise, compound, abandon, submit to arbitration, or otherwise settle any debt, account, claim or thing whatever relating to the testator's or intestate's estate or to the trust;

and for any of those purposes may enter into, give, execute, and do such agreements, instruments of composition or arrangements, releases, and other things as to him or them seem expedient, without being responsible for any loss occasioned by any act or thing so done by him or them in good faith.

18   Devolution of powers or trusts

(1) Where a power or trust is given to or imposed on two or more trustees jointly, the same may be exercised or performed by the survivors or survivor of them for the time being.

(2) Until the appointment of new trustees, the personal representatives or representative for the time being of a sole trustee, or, where there were two or more trustees of the last surviving or continuing trustee, shall be capable of exercising or performing any power or trust which was given to, or capable of being exercised by, the sole or last surviving or continuing trustee, or other the trustees or trustee for the time being of the trust.

(3) This section takes effect subject to the restrictions imposed in regard to receipts by a sole trustee, not being a trust corporation.

(4) In this section 'personal representative' does not include an executor who has renounced or has not proved.

23   Power to employ agents

(1) Trustees or personal representatives may, instead of acting personally, employ and pay an agent, whether a solicitor, banker, stockbroker, or other person, to transact any business or do any act required to be transacted or done in the execution of the trust, or the administration of the testator's or intestate's estate, including the receipt and payment of money, and shall be entitled to be allowed and paid all charges and expenses so incurred, and shall not be responsible for the default of any such agent if employed in good faith.

(2) Trustees or personal representatives may appoint any person to act as their agent or attorney for the purpose of selling, converting, collecting, getting in, and executing and perfecting assurances of, or managing or cultivating, or otherwise administering any property, real or personal, moveable or immoveable, subject to the trust or forming part of the testator's or intestate's estate, in any place outside the United Kingdom or executing or exercising any discretion or trust or power vested in them in relation to any such property, with such ancillary powers, and with the subject to such provisions and restrictions as they may think fit, including a power to appoint substitutes, and shall not, by reason only of their having made such appointment, be responsible for any loss arising thereby.

26 Protection against liability in respect of rents and covenants

(1) Where a personal representative or trustee liable as such for –

(a) any rent, covenant, or agreement reserved by or contained in any lease; or

(b) any rent, covenant or agreement payable under or contained in any grant made in consideration of a rentcharge; or

(c) any indemnity given in respect of any rent, covenant or agreement referred to in either of the foregoing paragraphs;

satisfies all liabilities under the lease or grant which may have accrued, and been claimed, up to the date of the conveyance hereinafter mentioned, and, where necessary, sets apart a sufficient fund to answer any future claim that may be made in respect of any fixed and ascertained sum which the lessee or grantee agreed to lay out on the property demised or granted, although the period for laying out the same may not have arrived, then and in any such case the personal representative or trustee may convey the property demised or granted to a purchaser, legatee, devisee, or other person entitled to call for a conveyance thereof and thereafter –

(i) he may distribute the residuary real and personal estate of the deceased testator or intestate or, as the case may be, the trust estate (other than the fund, if any, set apart as aforesaid) to or amongst the persons entitled thereto, without appropriating any part, or any further part, as the case may be, of the estate of the deceased or of the trust estate to meet any future liability under the said lease or grant;

(ii) notwithstanding such distribution, he shall not be personally liable in respect of any subsequent claim under the said lease or grant.

(2) This section operates without prejudice to the right of the lessor or grantor, or the persons deriving title under the lessor or grantor, to follow the assets of the deceased or the trust property into the hands of the persons amongst whom the same may have been respectively distributed, and applies notwithstanding anything to the contrary in the will or other instrument, if any, creating the trust.

(3) In this section 'lease' includes an underlease and an agreement for a lease or underlease and any instrument giving any such indemnity as aforesaid or varying the liabilities under the lease; 'grant' applies to a grant whether the rent is created by limitation, grant, reservation, or otherwise, and includes an agreement for a grant and any instrument giving any such indemnity as aforesaid or varying the liabilities under the grant; 'lessee' and 'grantee' include persons respectively deriving title under them.

27 Protection by means of advertisements

(1) With a view to the conveyance to or distribution among the persons entitled to any real or personal property, the trustees of a settlement or of a disposition on trust for sale or personal representatives, may give notice by advertisement in the Gazette, and in a newspaper circulating in the district in which the land is situated, and such other like notices, including notices elsewhere than in England and Wales, as would, in any special case, have been directed by a court of competent jurisdiction in an action for administration, of their intention to make such conveyance or distribution as aforesaid, and requiring any person interested to send to the trustees or personal representatives within the time, not being less than two months, fixed in the notice or, where more than one notice is given, in the last of the notices, particulars of his claim in respect of the property or any part thereof to which the notice relates.

(2) At the expiration of the time fixed by the notice the trustees or personal representatives may convey or distribute the property or any part thereof to which the notice relates, to or among the persons entitled thereto, having regard only to the claims, whether formal or not, of which the trustees or personal representatives then had

notice and shall not, as respects the property so conveyed or distributed, be liable to any person of whose claim the trustees or personal representatives have not had notice at the time of conveyance or distribution; but nothing in this section –

(a) prejudices the right of any person to follow the property, or any property representing the same, into the hands of any person, other than a purchaser, who may have received it; or

(b) frees the trustees or personal representatives from any obligation to make searches or obtain official certificates of search similar to those which an intending purchaser would be advised to make or obtain.

(3) This section applies notwithstanding anything to the contrary in the will or other instrument, if any, creating the trust.

30 Implied indemnity of trustees

(1) A trustee shall be chargeable only for money and securities actually received by him notwithstanding his signing any receipt for the sake of conformity, and shall be answerable and accountable only for his own acts, receipts, neglects, or defaults, and not for those of any other trustee, nor for any banker, broker, or other person with whom any trust money or securities may be deposited, nor for the insufficiency or deficiency of any securities nor for any other loss, unless the same happens through his own wilful default.

(2) A trustee may reimburse himself or pay or discharge out of the trust premises all expenses incurred in or about the execution of the trusts or powers.

36 Power of appointing new or additional trustees

(1) Where a trustee, either original or substituted, and whether appointed by a court or otherwise, is dead, or remains out of the United Kingdom for more than twelve months, or desires to be discharged from all or any of the trusts or powers reposed in or conferred on him, or refuses or is unfit to act therein, or is incapable of acting therein, or is an infant, then, subject to the restrictions imposed by this Act on the number of trustees, –

(a) the person or persons nominated for the purpose of appointing new trustees by the instrument, if any, creating the trust; or

(b) if there is no such person, or no such person able and willing to act, then the surviving or continuing trustees or trustee for the time being, or the personal representatives of the last surviving or continuing trustee;

may, by writing, appoint one or more other persons (whether or not being the persons exercising the power) to be a trustee or trustees in the place of the trustee so deceased, remaining out of the United Kingdom, desiring to be discharged, refusing, or being unfit or being incapable, or being an infant, as aforesaid.

(4) The power of appointment given by subsection (1) of this section or any similar previous enactment to the personal representatives of a last surviving or continuing trustee shall be and shall be deemed always to have been exercised by the executors for the time being (whether original or by representation) of such surviving or continuing trustee who have proved the will of their testator or by the administrators for the time being of such trustee without the concurrence of any executor who has renounced or has not proved.

(5) But a sole or last surviving executor intending to renounce, or all the executors where they all intend to renounce, shall have and shall be deemed always to have had power, at any time before renouncing probate, to exercise the power of appointment given by this section, or by any similar previous enactment, if willing to act for that purpose and without thereby accepting the office of executor ...

57 Power of court to authorise dealings with trust property

(1) Where in the management or administration of any property vested in trustees, any sale, lease, mortgage, surrender, release, or other disposition, or any purchase, investment, acquisition, expenditure, or other transaction, is in the opinion of the court expedient, but the same cannot be effected by reason of the absence of any power for that purpose vested in the trustees by the trust instrument, if any, or by law, the court may by order confer upon the trustees, either generally or in any particular instance, the necessary power for the purpose, on such terms, and subject to such provisions and conditions, if any, as the court may think fit and may direct in what manner any money authorised to be expended, and the costs of any transaction, are to be paid or borne as between capital and income.

(2) The court may, from time to time, rescind or vary any order made under this section, or may make any new or further order.

(3) An application to the court under this section may be made by the trustees, or by any of them, or by any person beneficially interested under the trust.

(4) This section does not apply to trustees of a settlement for the purposes of the Settled Land Act 1925.

61 Power to relieve trustee from personal liability

If it appears to the court that a trustee, whether appointed by the court or otherwise, is or may be personally liable for any breach of trust, whether the transaction alleged to be a breach of trust occurred before or after the commencement of this Act, but has acted honestly and reasonably, and ought fairly to be excused for the breach of trust and for omitting to obtain the directions of the court in the matter in which he committed such breach, then the court may relieve him either wholly or partly from personal liability for the same.

62 Power to make beneficiary indemnify for breach of trust

(1) Where a trustee commits a breach of trust at the instigation or request or with the consent in writing of a beneficiary, the court may, if it thinks fit, make such order as to the court seems just, for impounding all or any part of the interest of the beneficiary in the trust estate by way of indemnity to the trustee or persons claiming through him.

68 Definitions

In this Act, unless the context otherwise requires, the following expressions have the meanings hereby assigned to them respectively, that is to say –

(4) 'Gazette' means the London Gazette;

(9) 'Personal representative' means the executor, original or by representation, or administrator for the time being of a deceased person;

(17) 'Trust' does not include the duties incident to an estate conveyed by way of mortgage, but with this exception the expressions 'trust' and 'trustee' extend to implied and constructive trusts, and to cases where the trustee has a beneficial interest in the trust property, and to the duties incident to the office of a personal representative, and 'trustee' where the context admits, includes a personal representative.

As amended by the Law of Property (Amendment) Act 1926, ss7, 8(2), Schedule; Married Women (Restraint upon Anticipation) Act 1949, s1(4), Schedule 2.

LAW OF PROPERTY ACT 1925
(15 & 16 Geo 5 c 20)

PART I

GENERAL PRINCIPLES AS TO LEGAL ESTATES, EQUITABLE INTERESTS AND POWERS

33 Application of Part I to personal representatives

The provisions of this Part of this Act relating to trustees for sale apply to personal representatives holding on trust for sale, but without prejudice to their rights and powers for purposes of administration.

PART X

WILLS

175 Contingent and future testamentary gifts to carry the intermediate income

(1) A contingent or future specific devise or bequest of property, whether real or personal, and a contingent residuary devise of freehold land, and a specific or residuary devise of freehold land to trustees upon trust for persons whose interests are contingent or executory shall, subject to the statutory provisions relating to accumulations, carry the intermediate income of that property from the death of the testator, except so far as such income, or any part thereof, may be otherwise expressly disposed of.

176 Power for tenant in tail in possession to dispose of property by specific devise or bequest

(1) A tenant in tail of full age shall have power to dispose by will, by means of a devise or bequest referring specifically either to the property or to the instrument under which it was acquired or to entailed property generally –

(a) of all property of which he is tenant in tail in possession at his death; and

(b) of money (including the proceeds of property directed to be sold) subject to be invested in the purchase of property, of which if it had been so invested he would have been tenant in tail in possession at his death;

in like manner as if, after barring the entail, he had been tenant in fee simple or absolute owner thereof for an equitable interest at his death, but, subject to and in default of any such disposition by will, such property shall devolve in the same manner as if this section had not been passed.

(2) This section applies to entailed interests authorised to be created by this Act as well as to estates tail created before the commencement of this Act, but does not extend to a tenant in tail who is by statute restrained from barring or defeating his estate tail, whether the land or property in respect whereof he is so restrained was purchased with money provided by Parliament in consideration of public services or not, or to a tenant in tail after possibility of issue extinct, and does not render any interest which is not disposed of by the will of the tenant in tail liable for his debts or other liabilities.

(3) In this section 'tenant in tail' includes an owner of a base fee in possession who has power to enlarge the base fee into a fee simple without the concurrence of any other person.

179 Prescribed forms for reference in wills

The Lord Chancellor may from time to time prescribe and publish forms to which a testator may refer in his will, and give directions as to the manner in which they may be referred to, but, unless so referred to, such forms shall not be deemed to be incorporated in a will.

205 General definitions

(1) In this Act unless the context otherwise requires, the following expressions have the meanings hereby assigned to them respectively, that is to say ...

(ii) 'Conveyance' includes a mortgage, charge, lease, assent, vesting declaration, vesting instrument, disclaimer, release and every other assurance of property or of an interest therein by any instrument, except a will; 'convey' has a corresponding meaning; and 'disposition' includes a conveyance and also a devise, bequest, or an appointment of property contained in a will; and 'dispose of' has a corresponding meaning; ...

(viii) 'Instrument' does not include a statute, unless the statute creates a settlement;

(ix) 'Land' includes land of any tenure, and mines and minerals, whether or not held apart from the surface, buildings or parts of buildings (whether the division is horizontal, vertical or made in any other way) and other corporeal hereditaments; also a manor, an advowson, and a rent and other incorporeal hereditaments, and an easement, right, privilege, or benefit in, over, or derived from land; but not an undivided share in land; and 'mines and minerals' include any strata or seam of minerals or substances in or under any land, and powers of working and getting the same but not an undivided share thereof; and 'manor' includes a lordship, and reputed manor or lordship; and 'hereditament' means any real property which on an intestacy occurring before the commencement of this Act might have devolved upon an heir;

(x) 'Legal estates' means the estates, interests and charges, in or over land (subsisting or created at law) which are by this Act authorised to subsist or to be created as legal estates; 'equitable interests' means all the other interests and charges in or over land or in the proceeds of sale thereof; an equitable interest 'capable of subsisting as a legal estate' means such as could validly subsist or be created as a legal estate under this Act; ...

(xviii) 'Personal representative' means the executor, original or by representation, or administrator for the time being of a deceased person, and as regards any liability for the payment of death duties includes any person who takes possession of or intermeddles with the property of a deceased person without the authority of the personal representatives or the court;

(xix) 'Possession' includes receipt of rents and profits or the right to receive the same, if any; and 'income' includes rents and profits;

(xx) 'Property' includes any thing in action, and any interest in real or personal property;

(xxi) 'Purchaser' means a purchaser in good faith for valuable consideration and includes a lessee, mortgagee or other person who for valuable consideration acquires an interest in property except that in Part I of this Act and elsewhere where so expressly provided 'purchaser' only means a person who acquires an interest in or charge on property for money or money's worth; and in reference to a legal estate includes a chargee by way of legal mortgage; and where the context so requires 'purchaser' includes an intending purchaser; 'purchase' has a meaning corresponding with that of 'purchaser'; and 'valuable consideration' includes marriage but does not include a nominal consideration in money; ...

(xxix) 'Trust for sale', in relation to land, means an immediate binding trust for sale, whether or not exercisable at the request or with the consent of any person, and with or without a power at discretion to postpone the sale; 'trustees for sale' means the persons (including a personal representative) holding land on trust for sale; and 'power to postpone a sale' means power to postpone in the exercise of a discretion; ...

(xxxi) 'Will' includes codicil ...

(2) Where an equitable interest in or power over property arises by statute or operation of law, references to the creation of an interest or power include references to any interest or power so arising.

ADMINISTRATION OF ESTATES ACT 1925

(15 & 16 Geo 5 c 23)

PART I

DEVOLUTION OF REAL ESTATE

1 Devolution of real estate on personal representative

(1) Real estate to which a deceased person was entitled for an interest not ceasing on his death shall on his death, and notwithstanding any testamentary disposition thereof, devolve from time to time on the personal representative of the deceased, in like manner as before the commencement of this Act chattels real devolved on the personal representative from time to time of a deceased person.

(2) The personal representatives for the time being of a deceased person are deemed in law his heirs and assigns within the meaning of all trusts and powers.

(3) The personal representatives shall be the representatives of the deceased in regard to his real estate to which he was entitled for an interest not ceasing on his death as well as in regard to his personal estate.

2 Application to real estate of law affecting chattels real

(1) Subject to the provisions of this Act, all enactments and rules of law, and all jurisdiction of any court with respect to the appointment of administrators or to probate or letters of administration, or to dealings before probate in the case of chattels real, and with respect to costs and other matters in the administration of personal estate, in force before the commencement of this Act, and all powers, duties, rights, equities, obligations, and liabilities of a personal representative in force at the commencement of this Act with

respect to chattels real, shall apply and attach to the personal representative and shall have effect with respect to real estate vested in him, and in particular all such powers of disposition and dealing as were before the commencement of this Act exercisable as respects chattels real by the survivor or survivors of two or more personal representatives, as well as by a single personal representative, or by all the personal representatives together, shall be exercisable by the personal representatives or representative of the deceased with respect to his real estate.

(2) Where as respects real estate there are two or more personal representatives, a conveyance of real estate devolving under this Part of this Act shall not, save as otherwise provided as respects trust estates including settled land, be made without the concurrence therein of all such representatives or an order of the court, but where probate is granted to one or some of two or more persons named as executors, whether or not power is reserved to the other or others to prove, any conveyance of the real estate may be made by the proving executor or executors for the time being, without an order of the court, and shall be as effectual as if all the persons named as executors had concurred therein.

3   Interpretation of Part I

(1) In this Part of this Act 'real estate' includes –

(i) chattels real, and land in possession, remainder, or reversion, and every interest in or over land to which a deceased person was entitled at the time of his death; and

(ii) real estate held on trust (including settled land) or by way of mortgage or security, but not money to arise under a trust for sale of land, nor money secured or charged on land.

(2) A testator shall be deemed to have been entitled at his death to any interest in real estate passing under any gift contained in his will which operates as an appointment under a general power to appoint by will, or operates under the testamentary power conferred by statute to dispose of an entailed interest.

(3) An entailed interest of a deceased person shall (unless disposed of under the testamentary power conferred by statute) be deemed an interest ceasing on his death, but any further or other interest of the deceased in the same property in remainder or reversion which is capable of being disposed of by his will shall not be deemed to be an interest so ceasing.

(4) The interest of a deceased person under a joint tenancy where another tenant survives the deceased is an interest ceasing on his death.

PART II

EXECUTORS AND ADMINISTRATORS

5   Cesser of right of executor to prove

Where a person appointed executor by a will –

(i) survives the testator but dies without having taken out probate of the will; or

(ii) is cited to take out probate of the will and does not appear to the citation; or

(iii) renounces probate of the will;

his rights in respect of the executorship shall wholly cease, and the representation to the testator and the administration of his real and personal estate shall devolve and be committed in like manner as if that person had not been appointed executor.

6   Withdrawal of renunciation

(1) Where an executor who has renounced probate has been permitted, whether before or after the commencement of this Act, to withdraw the renunciation and prove the will, the probate shall take effect and be deemed always to have taken effect without prejudice to the previous acts and dealings of and notices to any other personal representative who has previously proved the will or taken out letters of administration, and a memorandum of the subsequent probate shall be endorsed on the original probate or letters of administration.

(2) This section applies whether the testator died before or after the commencement of this Act.

7   Executor of executor represents original testator

(1) An executor of a sole or last surviving executor of a testator is the executor of that testator.

This provision shall not apply to an executor who does not prove the will of his testator, and in the case of an executor who on his death leaves surviving him some other executor of his testator who afterwards proves the will of that testator, it shall cease to apply on such probate being granted.

(2) So long as the chain of such representation is unbroken, the last executor in the chain is the executor of every preceding testator.

(3) The chain of such representation is broken by –

(a) an intestacy; or

(b) the failure of a testator to appoint an executor; or

(c) the failure to obtain probate of a will;

but is not broken by a temporary grant of administration if probate is subsequently granted.

(4) Every person in the chain of representation to a testator –

(a) has the same rights in respect of the real and personal estate of that testator as the original executor would have had if living; and

(b) is, to the extent to which the estate whether real or personal of that testator has come to his hands, answerable as if he were an original executor.

8   Right of proving executors to exercise powers

(1) Where probate is granted to one or some of two or more persons named as executors, whether or not power is reserved to the others or other to prove, all the powers which are by law conferred on the personal representative may be exercised by the proving executor or executors for the time being and shall be as effectual as if all the persons named as executors had concurred therein.

(2) This section applies whether the testator died before or after the commencement of this Act.

9   Vesting of estate of intestate between death and grant of administration

Where a person dies intestate, his real and personal estate, until administration is granted in respect thereof, shall vest in the Probate Judge in the same manner and to the same extent as formerly in the case of personal estate it vested in the ordinary.

15 Executor not to act while administration is in force

Where administration has been granted in respect of any real or personal estate of a deceased person, no person shall have power to bring any action or otherwise act as executor of the deceased person in respect of the estate comprised in or affected by the grant until the grant has been recalled or revoked.

17 Continuance of legal proceedings after revocation of temporary administration

(1) If, while any legal proceeding is pending in any court by or against an administrator to whom a temporary administration has been granted, that administration is revoked, that court may order that the proceeding be continued by or against the new personal representative in like manner as if the same had been originally commenced by or against him, but subject to such conditions and variations, if any, as that court directs.

(2) The county court has jurisdiction under this section where the proceedings are pending in that court.

21 Rights and liabilities of administrator

Every person to whom administration of the real and personal estate of a deceased person is granted shall, subject to the limitations contained in the grant, have the same rights and liabilities and be accountable in like manner as if he were the executor of the deceased.

21A Debtor who becomes creditor's executor by representation or administrator to account for debt to estate

(1) Subject to subsection (2) of this section, where a debtor becomes his deceased creditor's executor by representation or administrator –

(a) his debt shall thereupon be extinguished; but

(b) he shall be accountable for the amount of the debt as part of the creditor's estate in any case where he would be so accountable if he had been appointed as an executor by the creditor's will.

(2) Subsection (1) of this section does not apply where the debtor's authority to act as executor or administrator is limited to part only of the creditor's estate which does not include the debt; and a debtor whose debt is extinguished by virtue of paragraph (a) shall not be accountable for its amount by virtue of paragraph (b) of that subsection in any case where the debt was barred by the Limitation Act 1939 before he became the creditor's executor or administrator.

(3) In this section 'debt' includes any liability, and 'debtor' and 'creditor' shall be construed accordingly.

22   Special executors as respects settled land

(1) A testator may appoint, and in default of such express appointment shall be deemed to have appointed, as his special executors in regard to settled land, the persons, if any, who are at his death the trustees of the settlement thereof, and probate may be granted to such trustees specially limited to the settled land.

In this subsection 'settled land' means land vested in the testator which was settled previously to his death and not by his will.

(2) A testator may appoint other persons either with or without such trustees as aforesaid or any of them to be his general executors in regard to his other property and assets.

23   Provisions where, as respects settled land, representation is not granted to the trustees of the settlement

(1) Where settled land becomes vested in a personal representative, not being a trustee of the settlement, upon trust to convey the land to or assent to the vesting thereof in the tenant for life or statutory owner in order to give effect to a settlement created before the death of the deceased and not by his will, or would, on the grant of representation to him, have become so vested, such representative may –

(a) before representation has been granted, renounce his office in regard only to such settled land without renouncing it in regard to other property;

(b) after representation has been granted, apply to the court for revocation of the grant in regard to the settled land without applying in regard to other property.

(2) Whether such renunciation or revocation is made or not, the trustees of the settlement, or any person beneficially interested thereunder, may apply to the High Court for an order appointing a special or additional personal representative in respect of the settled land, and a special or additional personal representative, if and when appointed under the order, shall be in the same position as if representation had originally been granted to him alone in place of the original personal representative, if any, or to him jointly with the original personal representative, as the case may be, limited to the settled land, but without prejudice to the previous acts and dealings, if any, of the personal representative originally constituted or the effect of notices given to such personal representative.

(3) The court may make such order as aforesaid subject to such security, if any, being given by or on behalf of the special or additional personal representative, as the court may direct, and shall, unless the court considers that special considerations apply, appoint such persons as may be necessary to secure that the persons to act as representatives in respect of the settled land shall, if willing to act, be the same persons as are the trustees of the settlement, and an office copy of the order when made shall be furnished to the principal registry of the Family Division of the High Court for entry, and a memorandum of the order shall be endorsed on the probate or administration.

(4) The person applying for the appointment of a special or additional personal representative shall give notice of the application to the principal registry of the Family Division of the High Court in the manner prescribed.

(5) Rules of court may be made for prescribing for all matters required for giving effect to the provisions of this section, and in particular –

(a) for notice of any application being given to the proper officer;

(b) for production of orders, probates, and administration to the registry;

(c) for the endorsement on a probate or administration of a memorandum of an order, subject or not to any exceptions;

(d) for the manner in which the costs are to be borne;

(e) for protecting purchasers and trustees and other persons in a fiduciary position, dealing in good faith with or giving notices to a personal representative before notice of any order has been endorsed on the probate or administration or a pending action has been registered in respect of the proceedings.

24 Power for special personal representatives to dispose of settled land

(1) The special personal representatives may dispose of the settled land without the concurrence of the general personal representatives, who may likewise dispose of the other property and assets of the deceased without the concurrence of the special personal representatives.

(2) In this section the expression 'special personal representatives' means the representatives appointed to act for the purposes of settled land and includes any original personal representative who is to act with an additional personal representative for those purposes.

25 Duty of personal representatives

The personal representative of a deceased person shall be under a duty to –

(a) collect and get in the real and personal estate of the deceased and administer it according to law;

(b) when required to do so by the court, exhibit on oath in the court a full inventory of the estate and when so required render an account of the administration of the estate to the court;

(c) when required to do so by the High Court, deliver up the grant of probate or administration to that court.

26 Right of personal representative to distrain for arrears of a rentcharge or rent

(3) A personal representative may distrain for arrears of a rentcharge due or accruing to the deceased in his lifetime on the land affected or charged therewith, so long as the land remains in the possession of the person liable to pay the rentcharge or of the persons deriving title under him, and in like manner as the deceased might have done had he been living.

(4) A personal representative may distrain upon land for arrears of rent due or accruing to the deceased in like manner as the deceased might have done had he been living.

Such arrears may be distrained for after the termination of the lease or tenancy as if the term or interest had not determined, if the distress is made –

(a) within six months after the termination of the lease or tenancy;

(b) during the continuance of the possession of the lessee or tenant from whom the arrears were due.

The statutory enactments relating to distress for rent apply to any distress made pursuant to this subsection.

27 Protection of persons acting on probate or administration

(1) Every person making or permitting to be made any payment or disposition in good faith under a representation shall be indemnified and protected in so doing, notwithstanding any defect or circumstance whatsoever affecting the validity of the representation.

(2) Where a representation is revoked, all payments and dispositions made in good faith to a personal representative under the representation before the revocation thereof are a valid discharge to the person making the same; and the personal representative who acted under the revoked representation may retain and reimburse himself in respect of any payments or dispositions made by him which the person to whom representation is afterwards granted might have properly made.

28 Liability of person fraudulently obtaining or retaining estate of deceased

If any person, to the defrauding of creditors or without full valuable consideration, obtains, receives or holds any real or personal estate of a deceased person or effects the release of any debt or liability due to the estate of the deceased, he shall be charged as executor in his own wrong to the extent of the real and personal estate received or coming to his hands, or the debt or liability released, after deducting –

(a) any debt for valuable consideration and without fraud due to him from the deceased person at the time of his death; and

(b) any payment made by him which might properly be made by a personal representative.

29 Liability of estate of personal representative

Where a person as personal representative of a deceased person (including an executor in his own wrong) wastes or converts to his own use any part of the real or personal estate of the deceased, and dies, his personal representative shall to the extent of the available assets of the defaulter be liable and chargeable in respect of such waste or conversion in the same manner as the defaulter would have been if living.

PART III

ADMINISTRATION OF ASSETS

32 Real and personal estate of deceased are assets for payments of debts

(1) The real and personal estate, whether legal or equitable, of a deceased person, to the extent of his beneficial interest therein, and the real and personal estate of which a deceased person in pursuance of any general power (including the statutory power to dispose of entailed interests) disposes by his will, are assets for payment of his debts (whether by specialty or simple contract) and liabilities, and any disposition by will inconsistent with this enactment is void as against the creditors, and the court shall, if necessary, administer the property for the purposes of the payment of the debts and liabilities.

This subsection takes effect without prejudice to the rights of incumbrancers.

(2) If any person to whom any such beneficial interest devolves or is given, or in whom any such interest vests, disposes thereof in good faith before an action is brought or process is sued out against him, he shall be personally liable for the value of the interest so disposed of by him, but that interest shall not be liable to be taken in execution in the action or under the process.

33 Trust for sale

(1) On the death of a person intestate as to any real or personal estate, such estate shall be held by his personal representatives –

(a) as to the real estate upon trust to sell the same; and

(b) as to the personal estate upon trust to call in sell and convert into money such part thereof as may not consist of money, with power to postpone such sale and conversion for such a period as the personal representatives, without being liable to account, may think proper, and so that any reversionary interest be not sold until it falls into possession, unless the personal representatives see special reason for sale, and so also that, unless required for purposes of administration owing to want of other assets, personal chattels be not sold except for special reason.

(2) Out of the net money to arise from the sale and conversion of such real and personal estate (after payment of costs), and out of the ready money of the deceased (so far as not disposed of by his will, if any), the personal representative shall pay all such funeral, testamentary and administration expenses, debts and other liabilities as are properly payable thereout having regard to the rules of administration contained in this Part of this Act, and out of the residue of the said money the personal representative shall set aside a fund sufficient to provide for any pecuniary legacies bequeathed by the will (if any) of the deceased.

(3) During the minority of any beneficiary or the subsistence of any life interest and pending the distribution of the whole or any part of the estate of the deceased, the personal representatives may invest the residue of the said money, or so much thereof as may not have been distributed, in any investments for the time being authorised by statute for the investment of trust money, with power, at the discretion of the personal representatives, to change such investments for others of a like nature.

(4) The residue of the said money and any investments for the time being representing the same, including (but without prejudice to the trust for sale) any part of the estate of the deceased which may be retained unsold and is not required for the administration purposes aforesaid, is in this Act referred to as 'the residuary estate of the intestate'.

(5) The income (including net rents and profits of real estate and chattels real after payment of rates, taxes, rent, costs of insurance, repairs and other outgoings properly attributable to income) of so much of the real and personal estate of the deceased as may not be disposed of by his will, if any, or may not be required for the administration purposes aforesaid, may, however such estate is invested, as from the death of the deceased, be treated and applied as income, and for that purpose any necessary apportionment may be made between tenant for life and remainderman.

(6) Nothing in this section affects the rights of any creditor of the deceased or the rights of the Crown in respect of death duties.

(7) Where the deceased leaves a will, this section has effect subject to the provisions contained in the will.

34   Administration of assets

(3) Where the estate of a deceased person is solvent his real and personal estate shall, subject to rules of court and the provisions hereinafter contained as to charges on property of the deceased, and to the provisions, if any, contained in his will, be applicable towards the discharge of the funeral, testamentary and administration expenses, debts and liabilities payable thereout in the order mentioned in Part II of the First Schedule to this Act.

35   Charges on property of deceased to be paid primarily out of the property charged

(1) Where a person dies possessed of, or entitled to, or, under a general power of appointment (including the statutory power to dispose of entailed interest) by his will disposes of, an interest in property, which at the time of his death is charged with the payment of money, whether by way of legal mortgage, equitable charge or otherwise (including a lien for unpaid purchase money), and the deceased has not by will deed or other document signified a contrary or other intention, the interest so charged shall, as between the different persons claiming through the deceased, be primarily liable for the payment of the charge; and every part of the said interest, according to its value, shall bear a proportionate part of the charge on the whole thereof.

(2) Such contrary or other intention shall not be deemed to be signified –

(a) by a general direction for the payment of debts or of all the debts of the testator out of his personal estate, or his residuary real and personal estate, or his residuary real estate; or

(b) by a charge of debts upon any such estate;

unless such intention is further signified by words expressly or by necessary implication referring to all or some part of the charge.

(3) Nothing in this section affects the right of a person entitled to the charge to obtain payment or satisfaction thereof either out of the other assets of the deceased or otherwise.

36 Effect of assent or conveyance by personal representative

(1) A personal representative may assent to the vesting, in any person who (whether by devise, bequest, devolution, appropriation or otherwise) may be entitled thereto, either beneficially or as a trustee or personal representative, of any estate or interest in real estate to which the testator or intestate was entitled or over which he exercised a general power of appointment by his will, including the statutory power to dispose of entailed interests, and which devolved upon the personal representative.

(2) The assent shall operate to vest in that person the estate or interest to which the assent relates, and, unless a contrary intention appears, the assent shall relate back to the death of the deceased.

(3) The statutory covenants implied by a person being expressed to convey as personal representative, may be implied in an assent in like manner as in a conveyance by deed.

(4) An assent to the vesting of a legal estate shall be in writing, signed by the personal representative, and shall name the person in whose favour it is given and shall operate to vest in that person the legal estate to which it relates; and an assent not in writing or not in favour of a named person shall not be effectual to pass a legal estate.

(5) Any person in whose favour an assent or conveyance of a legal estate is made by a personal representative may require that notice of the assent or conveyance be written or endorsed on or permanently annexed to the probate or letters of administration, at the cost of the estate of the deceased, and that the probate or letters of administration be produced, at the like cost, to prove that the notice has been placed thereon or annexed thereto.

(6) A statement in writing by a personal representative that he has not given or made an assent or conveyance in respect of a legal estate, shall, in favour of a purchaser, but without prejudice to any previous disposition made in favour of another purchaser deriving title mediately or immediately under the personal representative, be sufficient evidence that an assent or conveyance has not been

given or made in respect of the legal estate to which the statement relates, unless notice of a previous assent or conveyance affecting that estate has been placed on or annexed to the probate or administration.

A conveyance by a personal representative of a legal estate to a purchaser accepted in the faith of such a statement shall (without prejudice as aforesaid and unless notice of a previous assent or conveyance affecting that estate has been placed on or annexed to the probate or administration) operate to transfer or create the legal estate expressed to be conveyed in like manner as if no previous assent or conveyance had been made by the personal representative.

A personal representative making a false statement, in regard to any such matter, shall be liable in like manner as if the statement had been contained in a statutory declaration.

(7) An assent or conveyance by a personal representative in respect of a legal estate shall, in favour of a purchaser, unless notice of a previous assent or conveyance affecting that legal estate has been placed on or annexed to the probate or administration, be taken as sufficient evidence that the person in whose favour the assent or conveyance is given or made is the person entitled to have the legal estate conveyed to him, and upon the proper trusts, if any, but shall not otherwise prejudicially affect the claim of any person rightfully entitled to the estate vested or conveyed or any charge thereon.

(8) A conveyance of a legal estate by a personal representative to a purchaser shall not be invalidated by reason only that the purchaser may have notice that all the debts, liabilities, funeral, and testamentary or administration expenses, duties and legacies of the deceased have been discharged or provided for.

(9) An assent or conveyance given or made by a personal representative shall not, except in favour of a purchaser of a legal estate, prejudice the right of the personal representative or any other person to recover the estate or interest to which the assent or conveyance relates, or to be indemnified out of such estate or interest against any duties, debt or liability to which such estate or interest would have been subject if there had not been any assent or conveyance.

(10) A personal representative may, as a condition of giving an assent or making a conveyance, require security for the discharge of any such duties, debt, or liability, but shall not be entitled to postpone the giving of an assent merely by reason of the subsistence

of any such duties, debt or liability if reasonable arrangements have been made for discharging the same; and an assent may be given subject to any legal estate or charge by way of legal mortgage.

(11) This section shall not operate to impose any stamp duty in respect of an assent, and in this section 'purchaser' means a purchaser for money or money's worth.

(12) This section applies to assents and conveyances made after the commencement of this Act, whether the testator or intestate died before or after such commencement.

37 Validity of conveyance not affected by revocation of representation

(1) All conveyances of any interest in real or personal estate made to a purchaser either before or after the commencement of this Act by a person to whom probate or letters of administration have been granted are valid, notwithstanding any subsequent revocation or variation, either before or after the commencement of this Act, of the probate or administration.

(2) This section takes effect without prejudice to any order of the court made before the commencement of this Act, and applies whether the testator or intestate died before or after such commencement.

38 Right to follow property and powers of the court in relation thereto

(1) An assent or conveyance by a personal representative to a person other than a purchaser does not prejudice the rights of any person to follow the property to which the assent or conveyance relates, or any property representing the same, into the hands of the person in whom it is vested by the assent or conveyance, or of any other person (not being a purchaser) who may have received the same or in whom it may be vested.

(2) Notwithstanding any such assent or conveyance the court may, on the application of any creditor or other person interested –

  (a) order a sale, exchange, mortgage, charge, lease, payment, transfer or other transaction to be carried out which the court considers requisite for the purpose of giving effect to the rights of the persons interested;

(b) declare that the person, not being a purchaser, in whom the property is vested is a trustee for those purposes;

(c) give directions respecting the preparation and execution of any conveyance or other instrument or as to any other matter required for giving effect to the order;

(d) make any vesting order, or appoint a person to convey in accordance with the provisions of the Trustee Act 1925.

(3) This section does not prejudice the rights of a purchaser or a person deriving title under him, but applies whether the testator or intestate died before or after the commencement of this Act.

(4) The county court has jurisdiction under this section where the estate in respect of which the application is made does not exceed in amount or value the county court limit.

39 Powers of management

(1) In dealing with the real and personal estate of the deceased his personal representatives shall, for purposes of administration, or during a minority of any beneficiary or the subsistence of any life interest, or until the period of distribution arrives, have –

(i) the same powers and discretions, including power to raise money by mortgage or charge (whether or not by deposit of documents), as a personal representative had before the commencement of this Act, with respect to personal estate vested in him, and such power of raising money by mortgage may in the case of land be exercised by way of legal mortgage; and

(ii) all the powers, discretions and duties conferred or imposed by law on trustees holding land upon an effectual trust for sale (including power to overreach equitable interests and powers as if the same affected the proceeds of sale); and

(iii) all the powers conferred by statute on trustees for sale, and so that every contract entered into by a personal representative shall be binding on and be enforceable against and by the personal representative for the time being of the deceased, and may be carried into effect, or be varied or rescinded by him, and, in the case of a contract entered into by a predecessor, as if it had been entered into by himself.

(2) Nothing in this section shall affect the right of any person to require an assent or conveyance to be made.

(3) This section applies whether the testator or intestate died before or after the commencement of this Act.

40 Powers of personal representative for raising money, etc

(1) For giving effect to beneficial interests the personal representative may limit or demise land for a term of years absolute, with or without impeachment for waste, to trustees on usual trusts for raising or securing any principal sum and the interest thereon for which the land, or any part thereof, is liable, and may limit or grant a rentcharge for giving effect to any annual or periodical sum for which the land or the income thereof or any part thereof is liable.

(2) This section applies whether the testator or intestate died before or after the commencement of this Act.

41 Powers of personal representative as to appropriation

(1) The personal representative may appropriate any part of the real or personal estate, including things in action, of the deceased in the actual condition or state of investment thereof at the time of appropriation in or towards satisfaction of any legacy bequeathed by the deceased, or of any other interest or share in his property, whether settled or not, as to the personal representative may seem just and reasonable, according to the respective rights of the persons interested in the property of the deceased:

Provided that –

(i) an appropriation shall not be made under this section so as to affect prejudicially any specific devise or bequest;

(ii) an appropriation of property, whether or not being an investment authorised by law or by the will, if any, of the deceased for the investment of money subject to the trust, shall not (save as hereinafter mentioned) be made under this section except with the following consents –

(a) when made for the benefit of a person absolutely and beneficially entitled in possession, the consent of that person;

(b) when made in respect of any settled legacy share or interest, the consent of either the trustee thereof, if any (not being also the personal representative), or the person who may for the time being be entitled to the income:

If the person whose consent is so required as aforesaid is an infant or is incapable, by reason of mental disorder within the meaning of the Mental Health Act 1983, of managing and administering his property and affairs, the consent shall be given on his behalf by his parents or parent, testamentary or other guardian, or receiver, or if, in the case of an infant, there is no such parent or guardian, by the court on the application of his next friend;

(iii) no consent (save of such trustee as aforesaid) shall be required on behalf of a person who may come into existence after the time of appropriation, or who cannot be found or ascertained at that time;

(iv) if no receiver is acting for a person suffering from mental disorder, then, if the appropriation is of an investment authorised by law or by the will, if any, of the deceased for the investment of money subject to the trust, no consent shall be required on behalf of the said person;

(v) if, independently of the personal representative, there is no trustee of a settled legacy share or interest, and no person of full age and capacity entitled to the income thereof, no consent shall be required to an appropriation in respect of such legacy share or interest, provided that the appropriation is of an investment authorised as aforesaid.

(1A) The county court has jurisdiction under provision (ii) to subsection (1) of this section where the estate in respect of which the application is made does not exceed in amount or value the county court limit.

(2) Any property duly appropriated under the powers conferred by this section shall thereafter be treated as an authorised investment, and may be retained or dealt with accordingly.

(3) For the purposes of such appropriation, the personal representative may ascertain and fix the value of the respective parts of the real and personal estate and the liabilities of the deceased as he may think fit, and shall for that purpose employ a duly qualified valuer in any case where any such employment may be necessary; and may make any conveyance (including an assent) which may be requisite for giving effect to the appropriation.

(4) An appropriation made pursuant to this section shall bind all persons interested in the property of the deceased whose consent is not hereby made requisite.

(5) The personal representative shall, in making the appropriation, have regard to the rights of any person who may thereafter come into existence, or who cannot be found or ascertained at the time of appropriation, and of any other person whose consent is not required by this section.

(6) This section does not prejudice any other power of appropriation conferred by law or by the will (if any) of the deceased, and takes effect with any extended powers conferred by the will (if any) of the deceased, and where an appropriation is made under this section, in respect of a settled legacy, share or interest, the property appropriated shall remain subject to all trusts for sale and powers of leasing, disposition, and management or varying investments which would have been applicable thereto or to the legacy, share or interest in respect of which the appropriation is made, if no such appropriation had been made.

(7) If after any real estate has been appropriated in purported exercise of the powers conferred by this section, the person to whom it was conveyed disposes of it or any interest therein, then, in favour of a purchaser, the appropriation shall be deemed to have been made in accordance with the requirements of this section and after all requisite consents, if any, had been given.

(8) In this section, a settled legacy, share or interest includes any legacy, share or interest to which a person is not absolutely entitled in possession at the date of the appropriation, also an annuity, and 'purchaser' means a purchaser for money or money's worth.

(9) This section applies whether the deceased died intestate or not, and whether before or after the commencement of this Act, and extends to property over which a testator exercises a general power of appointment, including the statutory power to dispose of entailed interests, and authorises the setting apart of a fund to answer an annuity by means of the income of that fund or otherwise.

42 Power to appoint trustees of infants' property

(1) Where an infant is absolutely entitled under the will or on the intestacy of a person dying before or after the commencement of this Act (in this subsection called 'the deceased') to a devise or legacy, or to the residue of the estate of the deceased, or any share therein, and such devise, legacy, residue or share is not under the will, if any, of the deceased, devised or bequeathed to trustees for the infant, the personal representatives of the deceased may appoint a trust

corporation or two or more individuals not exceeding four (whether or not including the personal representatives or one or more of the personal representatives), to be the trustee or trustees of such devise, legacy, residue or share for the infant, and to be trustees of any land devised or any land being or forming part of such residue or share for the purposes of the Settled Land Act 1925, and of the statutory provisions relating to the management of land during a minority and may execute or do any assurance or thing requisite for vesting such devise, legacy, residue or share in the trustee or trustees so appointed.

On such appointment the personal representatives, as such, shall be discharged from all further liability in respect of such devise, legacy, residue, or share, and the same may be retained in its existing condition or state of investment, or may be converted into money, and such money may be invested in any authorised investment.

(2) Where a personal representative has before the commencement of this Act retained or sold any such devise, legacy, residue or share, and invested the same or the proceeds thereof in any investments in which he was authorised to invest money subject to the trust, then, subject to any order of the court made before such commencement, he shall not be deemed to have incurred any liability on that account, or by reason of not having paid or transferred the money or property into court.

43 Obligations of personal representative as to giving possession of land and powers of the court

(1) A personal representative, before giving an assent or making a conveyance in favour of any person entitled, may permit that person to take possession of the land, and such possession shall not prejudicially affect the right of the personal representative to take or resume possession nor his power to convey the land as if he were in possession thereof, but subject to the interest of any lessee, tenant or occupier in possession or in actual occupation of the land.

(2) Any person who as against the personal representative claims possession of real estate, or the appointment of a receiver thereof, or a conveyance thereof, or an assent to the vesting thereof, or to be registered as proprietor thereof under the Land Registration Act 1925, may apply to the court for directions with reference thereto, and the court may make such vesting or other order as may be deemed proper, and the provisions of the Trustee Act 1925, relating

to vesting orders and to the appointment of a person to convey, shall apply.

(3) This section applies whether the testator or intestate died before or after the commencement of this Act.

(4) The county court has jurisdiction under this section where the estate in respect of which the application is made does not exceed in amount or value the county court limit.

44 Power to postpone distribution

Subject to the foregoing provisions of this Act, a personal representative is not bound to distribute the estate of the deceased before the expiration of one year from the death.

PART IV

DISTRIBUTION OF RESIDUARY ESTATE

45 Abolition of descent to heir, curtesy, dower and escheat

(1) With regard to the real estate and personal inheritance of every person dying after the commencement of this Act, there shall be abolished –

(a) all existing modes rules and canons of descent, and of devolution by special occupancy or otherwise, of real estate, or of a personal inheritance, whether operating by the general law or by the custom of gavelkind or borough english or by any other custom of any county, locality, or manor, or otherwise howsoever; and

(b) tenancy by the curtesy and every other estate and interest of a husband in real estate as to which his wife dies intestate, whether arising under the general law or by custom or otherwise; and

(c) dower and freebench and every other estate and interest of a wife in real estate as to which her husband dies intestate, whether arising under the general law or by custom or otherwise: Provided that where a right (if any) to freebench or other like right has attached before the commencement of this Act which cannot be barred by a testamentary or other disposition made by the husband, such right shall, unless released, remain in force as an equitable interest; and

(d) escheat to the Crown or the Duchy of Lancaster or the Duke of Cornwall or to a mesne lord for want of heirs.

(2) Nothing in this section affects the descent or devolution of an entailed interest.

46 Succession to real and personal estate on intestacy

(1) The residuary estate of an intestate shall be distributed in the manner or be held on the trusts mentioned in this section, namely —

(i) If the intestate leaves a husband or wife, then in accordance with the following Table:

TABLE

If the intestate —

(1) leaves — (a) no issue, and (b) no parent, or brother or sister of the whole blood, or issue of a brother or sister of the whole blood	the residuary estate shall be held in trust for the surviving husband or wife absolutely.
(2) leaves issue (whether or not persons mentioned in sub-paragraph (b) above also survive)	the surviving husband or wife shall take the personal chattels absolutely and, in addition, the residuary estate of the intestate (other than the personal chattels) shall stand charged with the payment of a fixed net sum, free of death duties and costs, to the surviving husband or wife with interest thereon from the date of the death at such rate as the Lord Chancellor may specify by order until paid or appropriated, and, subject to providing for that sum and the interest thereon, the residuary estate (other than the personal chattels) shall be held — (a) as to one half upon trust for the surviving husband or wife

during his or her life, and, subject to such life interest, on the statutory trusts for the issue of the intestate, and

(b) as to the other half, on the statutory trusts for the issue of the intestate.

(3) leaves one or more of the following, that is to say, a parent, a brother or sister of the whole blood, or issue of a brother or sister of the whole blood, but leaves no issue

the surviving husband or wife shall take the personal chattels absolutely and, in addition, the residuary estate of the intestate (other than the personal chattels) shall stand charged with the payment of a fixed net sum, free of death duties and costs, to the surviving husband or wife with interest thereon from the date of the death at such rate as the Lord Chancellor may specify by order until paid or appropriated, and, subject to providing for that sum and the interest thereon, the residuary estate (other than the personal chattels) shall be held –

(a) as to one half in trust for the surviving husband or wife absolutely, and

(b) as to the other half –

(i) where the intestate leaves one parent or both parents (whether or not brothers or sisters of the intestate or their issue also survive) in trust for the parent absolutely or, as the case may be, for the two parents in equal shares absolutely,

(ii) where the intestate leaves no parent, on the statutory trusts for the brothers and sisters of the whole blood of the intestate.

The fixed net sums referred to in paragraphs (2) and (3) of this Table shall be of the amounts provided by or under section 1 of the Family Provision Act 1966.

(ii) If the intestate leaves issue but no husband or wife the residuary estate of the intestate shall be held on the statutory trusts for the issue of the intestate;

(iii) If the intestate leaves no husband or wife and no issue but both parents, then the residuary estate of the intestate shall be held in trust for the father and mother in equal shares absolutely;

(iv) If the intestate leaves no husband or wife and no issue but one parent, then the residuary estate of the intestate shall be held in trust for the surviving father or mother absolutely;

(v) If the intestate leaves no husband or wife and no issue and no parent, then the residuary estate of the intestate shall be held in trust for the following persons living at the death of the intestate, and in the following order and manner, namely –

First, on the statutory trusts for the brothers and sisters of the whole blood of the intestate; but if no person takes an absolutely vested interest under such trusts; then

Secondly, on the statutory trusts for the brothers and sisters of the half blood of the intestate; but if no person takes an absolutely vested interested under such trusts; then

Thirdly, for the grandparents of the intestate and, if more than one survive the intestate, in equal shares; but if there is no member of this class; then

Fourthly, on the statutory trusts for the uncles and aunts of the intestate (being brothers or sisters of the whole blood of a parent of the intestate); but if no person takes an absolutely vested interest under such trusts; then

Fifthly, on the statutory trusts for the uncles and aunts of the intestate (being brothers or sisters of the half blood of a parent of the intestate).

(vi) In default of any person taking an absolute interest under the foregoing provisions, the residuary estate of the intestate shall belong to the Crown or to the Duchy of Lancaster or to the Duke of Cornwall for the time being, as the case may be, as bona vacantia, and in lieu of any right to escheat.

The Crown or the said Duchy or the said Duke may (without prejudice to the powers reserved by section 9 of the Civil List Act 1910, or any other powers), out of the whole or any part of the property devolving on them respectively, provide, in accordance with the existing practice, for dependants, whether kindred or not, of the intestate, and other persons for whom the intestate might reasonably have been expected to make provision.

(1A) The power to make orders under subsection (1) above shall be exercisable by statutory instrument subject to annulment in pursuance of a resolution of either House of Parliament; and any such order may be varied or revoked by a subsequent order made under the power.

(2) A husband and wife shall for all purposes of distribution or division under the foregoing provisions of this section be treated as two persons.

(3) Where the intestate and the intestate's husband or wife have died in circumstances rendering it uncertain which of them survived the other and the intestate's husband or wife is by virtue of section 184 of the Law of Property Act 1925 deemed to have survived the intestate, this section shall, nevertheless, have effect as respects the intestate as if the husband or wife had not survived the intestate.

(4) The interest payable on the fixed net sum payable to a surviving husband or wife shall be primarily payable out of income.

47 Statutory trusts in favour of issue and other classes of relatives of intestate

(1) Where under this Part of this Act the residuary estate of an intestate, or any part thereof, is directed to be held on the statutory trusts for the issue of the intestate, the same shall be held upon the following trusts, namely –

(i) In trust, in equal shares if more than one, for all or any of the children or child of the intestate, living at the death of the intestate, who attain the age of twenty-one years or marry under that age, and for all or any of the issue living at the death of the intestate who attain the age of eighteen years or marry under that age of any child of the intestate who predeceases the intestate, such issue to take through all degrees, according to their stocks, in equal shares if more than one, the share which their parent would have taken if living at the death of the intestate, and so that no issue shall take whose parent is living at the death of the intestate and so capable of taking;

(ii) The statutory power of advancement, and the statutory

provisions which relate to maintenance and accumulation of surplus income, shall apply, but when an infant marries such infant shall be entitled to give valid receipts for the income of the infant's share or interest;

(iii) Where the property held on the statutory trusts for issue is divisible into shares, then any money or property which, by way of advancement or on the marriage of a child of the intestate, has been paid to such child by the intestate or settled by the intestate for the benefit of such child (including any life or less interest and including property covenanted to be paid or settled) shall, subject to any contrary intention expressed or appearing from the circumstances of the case, be taken as being so paid or settled in or towards satisfaction of the share of such child or the share which such child would have taken if living at the death of the intestate, and shall be brought into account, at a valuation (the value to be reckoned as at the death of the intestate), in accordance with the requirements of the personal representatives;

(iv) The personal representatives may permit any infant contingently interested to have the use and enjoyment of any personal chattels in such manner and subject to such conditions (if any) as the personal representatives may consider reasonable, and without being liable to account for any consequential loss.

(2) If the trusts in favour of the issue of the intestate fail by reason of no child or other issue attaining an absolutely vested interest –

(a) the residuary estate of the intestate and the income thereof and all statutory accumulations, if any, of the income thereof, or so much thereof as may not have been paid or applied under any power affecting the same, shall go, devolve and be held under the provisions of this Part of this Act as if the intestate had died without leaving issue living at the death of the intestate;

(b) references in this Part of this Act to the intestate 'leaving no issue' shall be construed as 'leaving no issue who attain an absolutely vested interest';

(c) references in this Part of this Act to the intestate 'leaving issue' or 'leaving a child or other issue' shall be construed as 'leaving issue who attain an absolutely vested interest'.

(3) Where under this Part of this Act the residuary estate of an intestate or any part thereof is directed to be held on the statutory trusts for any class of relatives of the intestate, other than issue of the intestate, the same shall be held on trusts corresponding to the

statutory trusts for the issue of the intestate (other than the provision for bringing any money or property into account) as if such trusts (other than as aforesaid) were repeated with the substitution of references to the members or member of that class for references to the children or child of the intestate.

(4) References in paragraph (i) of subsection (1) of the last foregoing section to the intestate leaving, or not leaving, a member of the class consisting of brothers or sisters of the whole blood of the intestate and issue of brothers or sisters of the whole blood of the intestate shall be construed as references to the intestate leaving, or not leaving, a member of that class who attains an absolutely vested interest.

47A Right of surviving spouse to have his own life interest redeemed

(1) Where a surviving husband or wife is entitled to a life interest in part of the residuary estate, and so elects, the personal representative shall purchase or redeem the life interest by paying the capital value thereof to the tenant for life, or the persons deriving title under the tenant for life, and the costs of the transaction; and thereupon the residuary estate of the intestate may be dealt with and distributed free from the life interest.

(3) An election under this section shall only be exercisable if at the time of the election the whole of the said part of the residuary estate consists of property in possession, but, for the purposes of this section, a life interest in property partly in possession and partly not in possession may be treated as consisting of two separate life interests in those respective parts of the property.

(3A) The capital value shall be reckoned in such manner as the Lord Chancellor may by order direct, and an order under this subsection may include transitional provisions.

(3B) The power to make orders under subsection (3A) above shall be exercisable by statutory instrument subject to annulment in pursuance of a resolution of either House of Parliament; and any such order may be varied or revoked by a subsequent order made under the power.

(5) An election under this section shall be exercisable only within the period of twelve months from the date on which representation with respect to the estate of the intestate is first taken out:

Provided that if the surviving husband or wife satisfies the court that the limitation to the said period of twelve months will operate unfairly –

(a) in consequence of the representation first taken out being probate of a will subsequently revoked on the ground that the will was invalid or,

(b) in consequence of a question whether a person had an interest in the estate, or as to the nature of an interest in the estate, not having been determined at the time when representation was first taken out, or

(c) in consequence of some other circumstances affecting the administration or distribution of the estate,

the court may extend the said period.

(6) An election under this section shall be exercisable, except where the tenant for life is the sole personal representative, by notifying the personal representative (or, where there are two or more personal representatives of whom one is the tenant for life, all of them except the tenant for life) in writing; and a notification in writing under this subsection shall not be revocable except with the consent of the personal representative.

(7) Where the tenant for life is the sole personal representative an election under this section shall not be effective unless written notice thereof is given to the Senior Registrar of the Family Division of the High Court within the period within which it must be made; and provision may be made by probate rules for keeping a record of such notices and making that record available to the public.

In this subsection the expression 'probate rules' means rules of court made under section 127 of the Supreme Court Act 1981.

(8) An election under this section by a tenant for life who is an infant shall be as valid and binding as it would be if the tenant for life were of age; but the personal representative shall, instead of paying the capital value of the life interest to the tenant for life, deal with it in the same manner as with any other part of the residuary estate to which the tenant for life is absolutely entitled.

(9) In considering for the purposes of the foregoing provisions of this section the question when representation was first taken out, a grant limited to settled land or to trust property shall be left out of account and a grant limited to real estate or to personal estate shall be left out of account unless a grant limited to the remainder of the estate has previously been made or is made at the same time.

48 Powers of personal representative in respect of interests of surviving spouse

(2) The personal representatives may raise –

(a) the fixed net sum or any part thereof and the interest thereon payable to the surviving husband or wife of the intestate on the security of the whole or any part of the residuary estate of the intestate (other than the personal chattels), so far as that estate may be sufficient for the purpose or the said sum and interest may not have been satisfied by an appropriation under the statutory power available in that behalf; and

(b) in like manner the capital sum, if any, required for the purchase or redemption of the life interest of the surviving husband or wife of the intestate, or any part thereof not satisfied by the application for that purpose of any part of the residuary estate of the intestate;

and in either case the amount, if any, properly required for the payment of the costs of the transaction.

49 Application to cases of partial intestacy

(1) Where any person dies leaving a will effectively disposing of part of his property, this Part of this Act shall have effect as respects the part of his property not so disposed of subject to the provisions contained in the will and subject to the following modifications –

(a) the requirements of section 47 of this Act as to bringing property into account shall apply to any beneficial interests acquired by any issue of the deceased under the will of the deceased, but not to beneficial interests so acquired by any other persons;

(aa) where the deceased leaves a husband or wife who acquires any beneficial interests under the will of the deceased (other than personal chattels specifically bequeathed) the references in this Part of this Act to the fixed net sum payable to a surviving husband or wife, and to interest on that sum, shall be taken as references to the said sum diminished by the value at the date of death of the said beneficial interests, and to interest on that sum as so diminished and, accordingly, where the said value exceeds the said sum, this Part of this Act shall have effect as if references to the said sum, and interest thereon, were omitted;

(b) the personal representative shall, subject to his rights and powers for the purposes of administration, be a trustee for the persons entitled under this Part of this Act in respect of the part of the estate not expressly disposed of unless it appears by the will that the personal representative is intended to take such part beneficially.

(2) References in the foregoing provisions of this section to beneficial interests acquired under a will shall be construed as including a reference to a beneficial interest acquired by virtue of the exercise by the will of a general power of appointment (including the statutory power to dispose of entailed interests), but not of a special power of appointment.

(3) For the purposes of paragraph (aa) in the foregoing provisions of this section the personal representative shall employ a duly qualified valuer in any case where such employment may be necessary.

(4) The references in subsection (3) of section 47A of this Act to property are references to property comprised in the residuary estate and, accordingly, where a will of the deceased creates a life interest in property in possession, and the remaining interest in that property forms part of the residuary estate, the said references are references to that remaining interest (which, until the life interest determines, is property not in possession).

50 Construction of documents

(1) References to any Statutes of Distribution in an instrument inter vivos made or in a will coming into operation after the commencement of this Act, shall be construed as references to this Part of this Act; and references in such an instrument or will to statutory next of kin shall be construed, unless the context otherwise requires, as referring to the persons who would take beneficially on an intestacy under the foregoing provisions of this Part of this Act.

(2) Trusts declared in an instrument inter vivos made, or in a will coming into operation, before the commencement of this Act by reference to the Statutes of Distribution, shall, unless the contrary thereby appears, be construed as referring to the enactments (other than the Intestates' Estates Act 1890) relating to the distribution of effects of intestates which were in force immediately before the commencement of this Act.

(3) In subsection (1) of this section the reference to this Part of this Act, or the foregoing provisions of this Part of this Act, shall in relation to an instrument inter vivos made, or a will or codicil coming into operation, after the coming into force of section 18 of the Family Law Reform Act 1987 (but not in relation to instruments inter vivos made or wills or codicils coming into operation earlier) be construed as including references to that section.

51   Savings

(3) Where an infant dies after the commencement of this Act without having been married, and independently of this subsection he would, at his death, have been equitably entitled under a settlement (including a will) to a vested estate in fee simple or absolute interest in freehold land, or in any property settled to devolve therewith or as freehold land, such infant shall be deemed to have had an entailed interest, and the settlement shall be construed accordingly.

(4) This Part of this Act does not affect the devolution of an entailed interest as an equitable interest.

52   Interpretation of Part IV

In this Part of this Act 'real and personal estate' means every beneficial interest (including rights of entry and reverter) of the intestate in real and personal estate which (otherwise than in right of a power of appointment or of the testamentary power conferred by statute to dispose of entailed interests) he could, if of full age and capacity, have disposed of by his will and references (however expressed) to any relationship between two persons shall be construed in accordance with s1 of the Family Law Reform Act 1987.

PART V

SUPPLEMENTAL

55   Definitions

In this Act, unless the context otherwise requires, the following expressions have the meanings hereby assigned to them respectively, that is to say –

(1) (i) 'Administration' means, with reference to the real and personal estate of a deceased person, letters of administration, whether general or limited, or with the will annexed or otherwise;

(ii) 'Administrator' means a person to whom administration is granted;

(v) 'Income' includes rents and profits;

(vi) 'Intestate' includes a person who leaves a will but dies intestate as to some beneficial interest in his real or personal estate;

(ix) 'Pecuniary legacy' includes an annuity, a general legacy, a demonstrative legacy so far as it is not discharged out of the designated property, and any other general direction by a testator for the payment of money, including all death duties free from which any devise, bequest, or payment is made to take effect;

(x) 'Personal chattels' mean carriages, horses, stable furniture and effects (not used for business purposes), motor cars and accessories (not used for business purposes), garden effects, domestic animals, plate, plated articles, linen, china, glass, books, pictures, prints, furniture, jewellery, articles of household or personal use or ornament, musical and scientific instruments and apparatus, wines, liquors and consumable stores, but do not include any chattels used at the death of the intestate for business purposes nor money or securities for money.

(xi) 'Personal representative' means the executor, original or by representation, or administrator for the time being of a deceased person, and as regards any liability for the payment of death duties includes any person who takes possession of or intermeddles with the property of a deceased person without the authority of the personal representatives or the court, and 'executor' includes a person deemed to be appointed executor as respects settled land;

(xiv) 'Probate' means the probate of a will;

(xv) 'Probate judge' means the President of the Family Division of the High Court;

(xviii) 'Purchaser' means a lessee, mortgagee or other person who in good faith acquires an interest in property for valuable consideration, also an intending purchaser and 'valuable consideration' includes marriage, but does not include a nominal consideration in money;

(xix) 'Real estate' save as provided in Part IV of this Act means real estate, including chattels real, which by virtue of Part I of this Act devolves on the personal representative of a deceased person;

(xx) 'Representation' means the probate of a will and administration, and the expression 'taking out representation' refers to the obtaining of the probate of a will or of the grant of administration;

(xxiii) 'Securities' includes stocks, funds, or shares;

(xxvii) 'Trust for sale', in relation to land, means an immediate binding trust for sale, whether or not exercisable at the request or with the consent of any person, and with or without a power at discretion to postpone the sale; and 'power to postpone a sale' means power to postpone in the exercise of a discretion;

(xxviii) 'Will' includes codicil.

(2) References to a child or issue living at the death of any person include a child or issue en ventre sa mere at the death.

(3) References to the estate of a deceased person include property over which the deceased exercises a general power of appointment (including the statutory power to dispose of entailed interests) by his will.

FIRST SCHEDULE

PART II

ORDER OF APPLICATION OF ASSETS WHERE THE ESTATE IS SOLVENT

1. Property of the deceased undisposed of by will, subject to the retention thereout of a fund sufficient to meet any pecuniary legacies.

2. Property of the deceased not specifically devised or bequeathed but included (either by a specific or general description) in a residuary gift, subject to the retention out of such property of a fund sufficient to meet any pecuniary legacies, so far as not provided for as aforesaid.

3. Property of the deceased specifically appropriated or devised or bequeathed (either by a specific or general description) for the payment of debts.

4. Property of the deceased charged with, or devised or bequeathed (either by a specific or general description) subject to a charge for the payment of debts.

5. The fund, if any, retained to meet pecuniary legacies.

6. Property specifically devised or bequeathed, rateably according to value.

7. Property appointed by will under a general power, including the statutory power to dispose of entailed interests, rateably according to value.

8. The following provisions shall also apply –

(a) The order of application may be varied by the will of the deceased.

As amended by the Intestates Estates Act 1952, ss1, 2, 3; Mental Health Act 1959, s149(1), Schedule 7, Pt I; Family Provision Act 1966, s1; Family Law Reform Act 1969, s3(2); Administration of Justice Act 1970, s1(6), Schedule 2, paras 3, 5; Administration of Estates Act 1971, s9; Administration of Justice Act 1977, ss28(1), (2), (3), 32(4), Schedule 5, Pt VI; Limitation Amendment Act 1980, s10; Supreme Court Act 1981, s152(1), Schedule 5; Mental Health Act 1983, s148, Schedule 4, para 7; County Courts Act 1984, s148(1), Schedule 2, Pt III, paras 11, 12, 13, 14; Family Law Reform Act 1987, s33(1), Schedule 2, paras 3, 4.

INTESTATES' ESTATES ACT 1952
(15 & 16 Geo 6 & 1 Eliz 2 c 64)

5 Rights of surviving spouse as respects the matrimonial home

The Second Schedule to this Act shall have effect for enabling the surviving husband or wife of a person dying intestate after the commencement of this Act to acquire the matrimonial home.

6 Interpretation and construction

(1) In this Part of this Act the expression 'intestate' has the meaning assigned to it by section 55 of the principal Act [ie the Administration of Estates Act 1925].

(2) The references in subsection (1) of section 50 of the principal Act (which relates to the construction of documents) to Part IV of that Act, or to the foregoing provisions of that Part, shall in relation to an instrument inter vivos made or a will coming into operation after the commencement of this Act, but not in relation to instruments inter vivos made or wills coming into operation earlier, be construed as including references to this Part of this Act and the Schedules to be read therewith.

SECOND SCHEDULE

RIGHTS OF SURVIVING SPOUSE AS RESPECTS THE MATRIMONIAL HOME

1. (1) Subject to the provisions of this Schedule, where the residuary estate of the intestate comprises an interest in a dwelling-house in which the surviving husband or wife was resident at the time of the intestate's death, the surviving husband or wife may require the personal representative, in exercise of the power conferred by section 41 of the principal Act (and with due regard requirements of that section as to valuation), to appropriate

interest in the dwelling-house in or towards satisfaction of any absolute interest of the surviving husband or wife in the real and personal estate of the intestate.

(2) The right conferred by this paragraph shall not be exercisable where the interest is –

(a) a tenancy which at the date of the death of the intestate was a tenancy which would determine within the period of two years from that date; or

(b) a tenancy which the landlord by notice given after that date could determine within the remainder of that period.

(3) Nothing in subsection (5) of section 41 of the principal Act (which requires the personal representative, in making an appropriation to any person under that section, to have regard to the rights of others) shall prevent the personal representative from giving effect to the right conferred by this paragraph.

(4) The reference in this paragraph to an absolute interest in the real and personal estate of the intestate includes a reference to the capital value of a life interest which the surviving husband or wife has under this Act elected to have redeemed.

(5) Where part of a building was, at the date of the death of the intestate, occupied as a separate dwelling, that dwelling shall for the purposes of this Schedule be treated as a dwelling-house.

2. Where –

(a) the dwelling-house forms part of a building and an interest in the whole of the building is comprised in the residuary estate; or

(b) the dwelling-house is held with agricultural land and an interest in the agricultural land is comprised in the residuary estate; or

(c) the whole or a part of the dwelling-house was at the time of the intestate's death used as a hotel or lodging house; or

(d) a part of the dwelling-house was at the time of the intestate's death used for purposes other than domestic purposes,

the right conferred by paragraph 1 of this Schedule shall not be exercisable unless the court, on being satisfied that the exercise of that right is not likely to diminish the value of assets in the residuary estate (other than the said interest in the dwelling-house) or make them more difficult to dispose of, so orders.

3. (1) The right conferred by paragraph 1 of this Schedule –

(a) shall not be exercisable after the expiration of twelve months from the first taking out of representation with respect to the intestate's estate;

(b) shall not be exercisable after the death of the surviving husband or wife;

(c) shall be exercisable, except where the surviving husband or wife is the sole personal representative, by notifying the personal representative (or, where there are two or more personal representatives of whom one is the surviving husband or wife, all of them except the surviving husband or wife) in writing.

(2) A notification in writing under paragraph (c) of the foregoing sub-paragraph shall not be revocable except with the consent of the personal representative; but the surviving husband or wife may require the personal representative to have the said interest in the dwelling-house valued in accordance with section 41 of the principal Act and to inform him or her of the result of that valuation before he or she decides whether to exercise the right.

(3) Subsection (9) of the section 47A added to the principal Act by section 2 of this Act shall apply for the purposes of the construction of the reference in this paragraph to the first taking out of representation, and the proviso to subsection (5) of that section shall apply for the purpose of enabling the surviving husband or wife to apply for an extension of the period of twelve months mentioned in this paragraph.

4. (1) During the period of twelve months mentioned in paragraph 3 of this Schedule the personal representative shall not without the written consent of the surviving husband or wife sell or otherwise dispose of the said interest in the dwelling-house except in the course of administration owing to want of other assets.

(2) An application to the court under paragraph 2 of this Schedule may be made by the personal representative as well as by the surviving husband or wife, and if, on an application under that paragraph, the court does not order that the right conferred by paragraph 1 of this Schedule shall be exercisable by the surviving husband or wife, the court may authorise the personal representative to dispose of the said interest in the dwelling-house within the said period of twelve months.

(3) Where the court under sub-paragraph (3) of paragraph 3 of this Schedule extends the said period of twelve months, the court may direct that this paragraph shall apply in relation to the extended period as it applied in relation to the original period of twelve months.

(4) This paragraph shall not apply where the surviving husband or wife is the sole personal representative or one of two or more personal representatives.

(5) Nothing in this paragraph shall confer any right on the surviving husband or wife as against a purchaser from the personal representative.

5. (1) Where the surviving husband or wife is one of two or more personal representatives, the rule that a trustee may not be a purchaser of trust property shall not prevent the surviving husband or wife from purchasing out of the estate of the intestate an interest in a dwelling-house in which the surviving husband or wife was resident at the time of the intestate's death.

(2) The power of appropriation under section 41 of the principal Act shall include power to appropriate an interest in a dwelling-house in which the surviving husband or wife was resident at the time of the intestate's death partly in satisfaction of an interest of the surviving husband or wife in the real and personal estate of the intestate and partly in return for a payment of money by the surviving husband or wife to the personal representative.

6. (1) Where the surviving husband or wife is a person of unsound mind or a defective, a requirement or consent under this Schedule may be made or given on his or her behalf by the committee or receiver, if any, or, where there is no committee or receiver, by the court.

(2) A requirement or consent made or given under this Schedule by a surviving husband or wife who is an infant shall be as valid and binding as it would be if he or she were of age; and, as respects an appropriation in pursuance of paragraph 1 of this Schedule, the provisions of section 41 of the principal Act as to obtaining the consent of the infant's parent or guardian, or of the court on behalf of the infant, shall not apply.

7. (1) Except where the context otherwise requires, references in this Schedule to a dwelling-house include references to any garden or portion of ground attached to and usually occupied with the

dwelling-house or otherwise required for the amenity or convenience of the dwelling-house.

(2) This Schedule shall be construed as one with Part IV of the principal Act.

HUMAN TISSUE ACT 1961
(9 & 10 Eliz 2 c 54)

1   Removal of parts of bodies for medical purposes

(1) If any person, either in writing at any time or orally in the presence of two or more witnesses during his last illness, has expressed a request that his body or any specified part of his body be used after his death for therapeutic purposes or for purposes of medical education or research, the person lawfully in possession of his body after his death may, unless he has reason to believe that the request was subsequently withdrawn, authorise the removal from the body of any part or, as the case may be, the specified part, for use in accordance with the request.

(2) Without prejudice to the foregoing subsection, the person lawfully in possession of the body of a deceased person may authorise the removal of any part from the body for use for the said purposes if, having made such reasonable enquiry as may be practicable, he has no reason to believe –

(a) that the deceased had expressed an objection to his body being so dealt with after his death, and had not withdrawn it; or

(b) that the surviving spouse or any surviving relative of the deceased objects to the body being so dealt with ...

(5) Where a person has reason to believe that an inquest may be required to be held on any body or that a post-mortem examination of any body may be required by the coroner, he shall not, except with the consent of the coroner, –

(a) give an authority under this section in respect of the body; or

(b) act on such an authority given by any other person.

(6) No authority shall be given under this section in respect of any body by a person entrusted with the body for the purpose only of its interment or cremation.

(7) In the case of a body lying in a hospital, nursing home or other institution, any authority under this section may be given on behalf of the person having the control and management thereof by any officer or person designated for that purpose by the first-mentioned person.

(8) Nothing in this section shall be construed as rendering unlawful any dealing with, or with any part of, the body of a deceased person which is lawful apart from this Act ...

WILLS ACT 1963
(1963 c 44)

1   General rule as to formal validity

A will shall be treated as properly executed if its execution conformed to the internal law in force in the territory where it was executed, or in the territory where, at the time of its execution or of the testator's death, he was domiciled or had his habitual residence, or in a state of which, at either of those times, he was a national.

2   Additional rules

(1) Without prejudice to the preceding section, the following shall be treated as properly executed –

(a) a will executed on board a vessel or aircraft of any description, if the execution of the will conformed to the internal law in force in the territory with which, having regard to its registration (if any) and other relevant circumstances, the vessel or aircraft may be taken to have been most closely connected;

(b) a will so far as it disposes of immovable property, if its execution conformed to the internal law in force in the territory where the property was situated;

(c) a will so far as it revokes a will which under this Act would be treated as properly executed or revokes a provision which under this Act would be treated as comprised in a properly executed will, if the execution of the later will conformed to any law by reference to which the revoked will or provision would be so treated;

(d) a will so far as it exercises a power of appointment, if the execution of the will conformed to the law governing the essential validity of the power.

(2) A will so far as it exercises a power of appointment shall not be treated as improperly executed by reason only that its execution was not in accordance with any formal requirements contained in the instrument creating the power.

3   Certain requirements to be treated as formal

Where (whether in pursuance of this Act or not) a law in force outside the United Kingdom falls to be applied in relation to a will, any requirement of that law whereby special formalities are to be observed by testators answering a particular description, or witnesses to the execution of a will are to possess certain qualifications, shall be treated, notwithstanding any rule of that law to the contrary, as a formal requirement only.

4   Construction of wills

The construction of a will shall not be altered by reason of any change in the testator's domicile after the execution of the will.

6   Interpretation

(1) In this Act –

'internal law' in relation to any territory or state means the law which would apply in a case where no question of the law in force in any other territory or state arose;

'state' means a territory or group of territories having its own law of nationality;

'will' includes any testamentary instrument or act, and 'testator' shall be construed accordingly.

(2) Where under this Act the internal law in force in any territory or state is to be applied in the case of a will, but there are in force in that territory or state two or more systems of internal law relating to the formal validity of wills, the system to be applied shall be ascertained as follows –

(a) if there is in force throughout the territory or state a rule indicating which of those systems can properly be applied in the case in question, that rule shall be followed; or

(b) if there is no such rule, the system shall be that with which the testator was most closely connected at the relevant time, and for this purpose the relevant time is the time of the testator's death where the matter is to be determined by reference to circumstances prevailing at his death, and the time of execution of the will in any other case.

(3) In determining for the purposes of this Act whether or not the execution of a will conformed to a particular law, regard shall be had to the formal requirements of that law at the time of execution, but this shall not prevent account being taken of an alteration of law affecting wills executed at that time if the alteration enables the will to be treated as properly executed.

7 Short title, commencement, repeal and extent

(2) This Act shall come into operation on 1 January 1964.

(4) This Act shall not apply to a will of a testator who died before the time of the commencement of this Act and shall apply to a will of a testator who dies after that time whether the will was executed before or after that time ...

ADMINISTRATION OF ESTATES (SMALL PAYMENTS) ACT 1965
(1965 c 32)

1 Increase in amounts disposable on death without representation

(1) In the enactments and instruments listed in Schedule 1 to this Act, of which –

(a) those listed in Part I are enactments authorising the disposal of property on death, without the necessity for probate or other proof of title, to persons appearing to be beneficially entitled thereto, to relatives or dependants of the deceased or to other persons described in the enactments, but subject to a limit which is in most cases £100 and which does not in any case exceed £100;

(b) those listed in Part II are enactments giving power to make rules or regulations containing corresponding provisions subject to a limit of £100; and

(c) those listed in Part III are such rules and regulations as aforesaid and instruments containing corresponding provisions made under other enactments and containing a limit which does not in any case exceed £200;

the said limit shall, subject to the provisions of that Schedule, in each case be £5,000 instead of the limit specified in the enactment or instrument; and for references to the said limits in those enactments and instruments there shall accordingly be substituted references to £5,000.

2 Increase in amounts disposable on death by nomination

(1) In the enactments and instrument listed in Schedule 2 to this Act (which enable a person by nomination to dispose of property on

his death up to a limit of £100 or, in some cases, £200) the said limit shall, subject to the provisions of that Schedule, in each case be £5,000 instead of the limit specified in the enactments or instrument; and for references to the said limits in the said enactments and instrument there shall accordingly be substituted references to £5,000.

(2) This section shall apply in relation to any nomination delivered at or sent to the appropriate office, or made in the appropriate book, after the expiration of a period of one month beginning with the date on which this Act is passed.

3　Extension of certain enactments relating to intestacies to cases where deceased leaves a will

(1) The enactments mentioned in Schedule 3 to this Act (all of which are listed in Part I of Schedule 1 to this Act) shall have effect subject to the amendments in that Schedule, which are amendments extending the operation of those enactments to cases where the deceased leaves a will.

6　Power to provide for further increases

(1) The Treasury may from time to time by order direct that –

(a) sections 1 and 2 of this Act, so far as they relate to any enactment; and

(b) section 68 of the Friendly Societies Act 1974 (which contains provisions similar to the enactments to which section 1 of this Act relates but subject to a limit of £500); and

(d) section 6(1) of the National Debt Act 1972; and

(e) sections 66 and 67 of the said Act of 1974 (which contain provisions similar to the enactments to which section 2 of this Act relates but subject to a limit of £500);

shall have effect as if for references to £500 there were substituted references to such higher amount as may be specified in the order.

SCHEDULE 1

STATUTORY PROVISIONS AUTHORISING DISPOSAL OF PROPERTY ON DEATH WITHOUT REPRESENTATION

PART I

ENACTMENTS

[In addition to a number of public and private Acts of limited importance, the following Acts are amended –

The Loan Societies Act 1840

The Navy and Marines (Property of Deceased) Act 1865

The Regimental Debts Act 1893

The Superannuation (Ecclesiastical Commissioners and Queen Anne's Bounty) Act 1914

The Government Annuities Act 1929

The Superannuation (Various Services) Act 1938

The Local Government Superannuation Act 1953

The Industrial and Provident Societies Act 1965]

PART II

ENABLING ENACTMENTS

The Pensions and Yeomanry Pay Act 1884

The Elementary School Teachers (Superannuation) Act 1898

PART III

INSTRUMENTS

[Certain statutory instruments are amended]

SCHEDULE 2

STATUTORY PROVISIONS AUTHORISING DISPOSAL OF PROPERTY ON DEATH BY NOMINATION

[Certain local and other Acts are amended]

SCHEDULE 3

EXTENSION OF ENACTMENTS RELATING TO INTESTACIES

[In addition to certain private Acts, the following Acts are extended –

The Loan Societies Act 1840

The Industrial and Provident Societies Act 1965]

As amended by the Merchant Shipping Act 1970, s100(1), Schedule 3, para 11; National Debt Act 1972, s6(3); Friendly Societies Act 1974, s116(1), Schedule 9, para 20; Administration of Estates (Small Payments) (Increase of Limit) Order 1984; Statute Law (Repeals) Act 1993, s1(1), Schedule 1, Pt IX.

FAMILY PROVISION ACT 1966
(1966 c 35)

1 Increase of net sum payable to surviving husband or wife on intestacy

(1) In the case of a person dying after the coming into force of this section, section 46(1) of the Administration of Estates Act 1925, as amended by section 1 of the Intestates' Estates Act 1952 and set out in Schedule 1 to that Act, shall apply as if the net sums charged by paragraph (i) on the residuary estate in favour of a surviving husband or wife were as follows, that is to say –

(a) under paragraph (2) of the Table (which charges a net sum ... where the intestate leaves issue) a sum of £125,000 or of such larger amount as may from time to time be fixed by order of the Lord Chancellor; and

(b) under paragraph (3) of the Table (which charges a net sum ... where the intestate leaves certain close relatives but no issue) a sum of £200,000 or of such larger amount as may from time to time be so fixed.

As amended by the Family Provision (Intestate Succession) Order 1993 as respects persons dying after 1 December 1993.

WILLS ACT 1968
(1968 c 28)

1 Restriction of operation of Wills Act 1837, s15

(1) For the purposes of section 15 of the Wills Act 1837 (avoidance of gifts to attesting witnesses and their spouses) the attestation of a will by a person to whom or to whose spouse there is given or made any such disposition as is described in that section shall be disregarded if the will is duly executed without his attestation and without that of any other such person.

(2) This section applies to the will of any person dying after the passing of this Act, whether executed before or after the passing of this Act.

FAMILY LAW REFORM ACT 1969
(1969 c 46)

3 Provisions relating to wills and intestacy

(3) Any will which –

(a) has been made, whether before or after the coming into force of this section, by a person under the age of eighteen; and

(b) is valid by virtue of the provisions of section 11 of the [Wills Act] 1837 and the [Wills (Soldiers and Sailors) Act] 1918,

may be revoked by that person notwithstanding that he is still under that age whether or not the circumstances are then such that he would be entitled to make a valid will under those provisions.

(4) In this section 'will' has the same meaning as in the said Act of 1837 and 'intestate' has the same meaning as in the [Administration of Estates Act] 1925.

ADMINISTRATION OF ESTATES ACT 1971
(1971 c 25)

10 Retainer, preference and the payment of debts by personal representatives

(1) The right of retainer of a personal representative and his right to prefer creditors are hereby abolished.

(2) Nevertheless a personal representative –

(a) other than one mentioned in paragraph (b) below, who, in good faith and at a time when he has no reason to believe that the deceased's estate is insolvent, pays the debt of any person (including himself) who is a creditor of the estate; or

(b) to whom letters of administration had been granted solely by reason of his being a creditor and who, in good faith and at such a time pays the debt of another person who is a creditor of the estate;

shall not, if it subsequently appears that the estate is insolvent, be liable to account to a creditor of the same degree as the paid creditor for the sum so paid.

INHERITANCE (PROVISION FOR FAMILY AND DEPENDANTS) ACT 1975

(1975 c 63)

1 Application for financial provision from deceased's estate

(1) Where after the commencement of this Act a person dies domiciled in England and Wales and is survived by any of the following persons –

(a) the wife or husband of the deceased;

(b) a former wife or former husband of the deceased who has not remarried;

(c) a child of the deceased;

(d) any person (not being a child of the deceased) who, in the case of any marriage to which the deceased was at any time a party, was treated by the deceased as a child of the family in relation to that marriage;

(e) any person (not being a person included in the foregoing paragraphs of this subsection) who immediately before the death of the deceased was being maintained, either wholly or partly, by the deceased;

that person may apply to the court for an order under section 2 of this Act on the ground that the disposition of the deceased's estate effected by his will or the law relating to intestacy, or the combination of his will and that law, is not such as to make reasonable financial provision for the applicant.

(2) In this Act 'reasonable financial provision' –

(a) in the case of an application made by virtue of subsection (1)(a) above by the husband or wife of the deceased (except where the marriage with the deceased was the subject of a decree of judicial separation and at the date of death the decree was in force and the separation was continuing), means such financial provision as it would be reasonable in all the circumstances of the case for a husband or wife to receive, whether or not that provision is required for his or her maintenance;

(b) in the case of any other application made by virtue of subsection (1) above, means such financial provision as it would be reasonable in all the circumstances of the case for the applicant to receive for his maintenance.

(3) For the purposes of subsection (1)(e) above, a person shall be treated as being maintained by the deceased, either wholly or partly, as the case may be, if the deceased, otherwise than for full valuable consideration, was making a substantial contribution in money or money's worth towards the reasonable needs of that person.

2   Powers of court to make orders

(1) Subject to the provisions of this Act, where an application is made for an order under this section, the court may, if it is satisfied that the disposition of the deceased's estate effected by his will or the law relating to intestacy, or the combination of his will and that law, is not such as to make reasonable financial provision for the applicant, make any one or more of the following orders –

(a) an order for the making to the applicant out of the net estate of the deceased of such periodical payments and for such term as may be specified in the order;

(b) an order for the payment to the applicant out of that estate of a lump sum of such amount as may be so specified;

(c) an order for the transfer to the applicant of such property comprised in that estate as may be so specified;

(d) an order for the settlement for the benefit of the applicant of such property comprised in that estate as may be so specified;

(e) an order for the acquisition out of property comprised in that estate of such property as may be so specified and for the transfer of the property so acquired to the applicant or for the settlement thereof for his benefit;

(f) an order varying any ante-nuptial or post-nuptial settlement (including such a settlement made by will) made on the parties to a marriage to which the deceased was one of the parties, the variation being for the benefit of the surviving party to that marriage, or any child of that marriage, or any person who was treated by the deceased as a child of the family in relation to that marriage.

(2) An order under subsection (1)(a) above providing for the making out of the net estate of the deceased of periodical payments may provide for –

(a) payments of such amount as may be specified in the order,

(b) payments equal to the whole of the income of the net estate or of such portion thereof as may be so specified,

(c) payments equal to the whole of the income of such part of the net estate as the court may direct to be set aside or appropriated for the making out of the income thereof of payments under this section,

or may provide for the amount of the payments or any of them to be determined in any other way the court thinks fit.

(3) Where an order under subsection (1)(a) above provides for the making of payments of an amount specified in the order, the order may direct that such part of the net estate as may be so specified shall be set aside or appropriated for the making out of the income thereof of those payments; but no larger part of the net estate shall be so set aside or appropriated than is sufficient, at the date of the order, to produce by the income thereof the amount required for the making of those payments.

(4) An order under this section may contain such consequential and supplemental provisions as the court thinks necessary or expedient for the purpose of giving effect to the order or for the purpose of securing that the order operates fairly as between one beneficiary of the estate of the deceased and another and may, in particular, but without prejudice to the generality of this subsection –

(a) order any person who holds any property which forms part of the net estate of the deceased to make such payment or transfer such property as may be specified in the order;

(b) vary the disposition of the deceased's estate effected by the will or the law relating to intestacy, or by both the will and the law relating to intestacy, in such manner as the court thinks fair and reasonable having regard to the provisions of the order and all the circumstances of the case;

(c) confer on the trustees of any property which is the subject of an order under this section such powers as appear to the court to be necessary or expedient.

3 Matters to which court is to have regard in exercising powers under s2

(1) Where an application is made for an order under section 2 of this Act, the court shall, in determining whether disposition of the deceased's estate effected by his will or the law relating to intestacy, or the combination of his will and that law, is such as to make reasonable financial provision for the applicant and, if the court considers that reasonable financial provision has not been made, in determining whether and in what manner it shall exercise its powers under that section, have regard to the following matters, that is to say –

(a) the financial resources and financial needs which the applicant has or is likely to have in the foreseeable future;

(b) the financial resources and financial needs which any other applicant for an order under section 2 of this Act has or is likely to have in the foreseeable future;

(c) the financial resources and financial needs which any beneficiary of the estate of the deceased has or is likely to have in the foreseeable future;

(d) any obligations and responsibilities which the deceased had towards any applicant for an order under the said section 2 or towards any beneficiary of the estate of the deceased;

(e) the size and nature of the net estate of the deceased;

(f) any physical or mental disability of any applicant for an order under the said section 2 or any beneficiary of the estate of the deceased;

(g) any other matter, including the conduct of the applicant or any other person, which in the circumstances of the case the court may consider relevant.

(2) Without prejudice to the generality of paragraph (g) of subsection (1) above, where an application for an order under section 2 of this Act is made by virtue of section 1(1)(a) or 1(1)(b) of this Act, the court shall, in addition to the matters specifically mentioned in paragraphs (a) to (f) of that subsection, have regard to –

(a) the age of the applicant and the duration of the marriage;

(b) the contribution made by the applicant to the welfare of the family of the deceased, including any contribution made by looking after the home or caring for the family;

and, in the case of an application by the wife or husband of the deceased, the court shall also, unless at the date of death a decree of judicial separation was in force and the separation was continuing, have regard to the provision which the applicant might reasonably have expected to receive if on the day on which the deceased died the marriage, instead of being terminated by death, had been terminated by a decree of divorce.

(3) Without prejudice to the generality of paragraph (g) of subsection (1) above, where an application for an order under section 2 of this Act is made by virtue of section 1(1)(c) or 1(1)(d) of this Act, the court shall, in addition to the matters specifically mentioned in paragraphs (a) to (f) of that subsection, have regard to the manner in which the applicant was being or in which he might expect to be educated or trained, and where the application is made by virtue of section 1(1)(d) the court shall also have regard –

(a) to whether the deceased had assumed any responsibility for the applicant's maintenance and, if so, to the extent to which and the basis upon which the deceased assumed that responsibility and to the length of time for which the deceased discharged that responsibility;

(b) to whether in assuming and discharging that responsibility the deceased did so knowing that the applicant was not his own child;

(c) to the liability of any other person to maintain the applicant.

(4) Without prejudice to the generality of paragraph (g) of subsection (1) above, where an application for an order under section 2 of this Act is made by virtue of section 1(1)(e) of this Act, the court shall, in addition to the matters specifically mentioned in paragraphs (a) to (f) of that subsection, have regard to the extent to which and the basis upon which the deceased assumed responsibility for the maintenance of the applicant, and to the length of time for which the deceased discharged that responsibility.

(5) In considering the matters to which the court is required to have regard under this section, the court shall take into account the facts as known to the court at the date of the hearing.

(6) In considering the financial resources of any person for the purposes of this section the court shall take into account his earning capacity and in considering the financial needs of any person for the purposes of this section the court shall take into account his financial obligations and responsibilities.

4 Time-limit for applications

An application for an order under section 2 of this Act shall not, except with the permission of the court, be made after the end of the period of six months from the date on which representation with respect to the estate of the deceased is first taken out.

5 Interim orders

(1) Where on an application for an order under section 2 of this Act it appears to the court –

   (a) that the applicant is in immediate need of financial assistance, but it is not yet possible to determine what order (if any) should be made under that section; and

   (b) that property forming part of the net estate of the deceased is or can be made available to meet the need of the applicant;

the court may order that, subject to such conditions or restrictions, if any, as the court may impose and to any further order of the court, there shall be paid to the applicant out of the net estate of the deceased such sum or sums and (if more than one) at such intervals as the court thinks reasonable; and the court may order that, subject to the provisions of this Act, such payments are to be made until such date as the court may specify, not being later than the date on which the court either makes an order under the said section 2 or decides not to exercise its powers under that section.

(2) Subsections (2), (3) and (4) of section 2 of this Act shall apply in relation to an order under this section as they apply in relation to an order under that section.

(3) In determining what order, if any, should be made under this section the court shall, so far as the urgency of the case admits, have regard to the same matters as those to which the court is required to have regard under section 3 of this Act.

(4) An order made under section 2 of this Act may provide that any sum paid to the applicant by virtue of this section shall be treated to such an extent and in such manner as may be provided by that order as having been paid on account of any payment provided for by that order.

6 Variation, discharge, etc of orders for periodical payments

(1) Subject to the provisions of this Act, where the court has made an order under section 2(1)(a) of this Act (in this section referred to as 'the original order') for the making of periodical payments to any person (in this section referred to as 'the original recipient'), the court, on an application under this section, shall have power by order to vary or discharge the original order or to suspend any provision of it temporarily and to revive the operation of any provision so suspended.

(2) Without prejudice to the generality of subsection (1) above, an order made on an application for the variation of the original order may –

(a) provide for the making out of any relevant property of such periodical payments and for such term as may be specified in the order to any person who has applied, or would but for section 4 of this Act be entitled to apply, for an order under section 2 of this Act (whether or not, in the case of any application, an order was made in favour of the applicant);

(b) provide for the payment out of any relevant property of a lump sum of such amount as may be so specified to the original recipient or to any such person as is mentioned in paragraph (a) above;

(c) provide for the transfer of the relevant property, or such part thereof as may be so specified, to the original recipient or to any such person as is so mentioned.

(3) Where the original order provides that any periodical payments payable thereunder to the original recipient are to cease on the occurrence of an event specified in the order (other than the remarriage of a former wife or former husband) or on the expiration of a period so specified, then, if, before the end of the period of six months from the date of the occurrence of that event or of the expiration of that period, an application is made for an order under this section, the court shall have power to make any order which it would have had power to make if the application had been made before the date (whether in favour of the original recipient or any such person as is mentioned in subsection (2)(a) above and whether having effect from that date or from such later date as the court may specify).

(4) Any reference in this section to the original order shall include a reference to an order made under this section and any reference in this section to the original recipient shall include a reference to any person to whom periodical payments are required to be made by virtue of an order under this section.

(5) An application under this section may be made by any of the following persons, that is to say –

(a) any person who by virtue of section 1(1) of this Act has applied, or would but for section 4 of this Act be entitled to apply, for an order under section 2 of this Act,

(b) the personal representatives of the deceased,

(c) the trustees of any relevant property, and

(d) any beneficiary of the estate of the deceased.

(6) An order under this section may only affect –

(a) property the income of which is at the date of the order applicable wholly or in part for the making of the periodical payments to any person who has applied for an order under this Act, or

(b) in the case of an application under subsection (3) above in respect of payments which have ceased to be payable on the occurrence of an event or the expiration of a period, property the income of which was so applicable immediately before the occurrence of that event or the expiration of that period, as the case may be,

and any such property as is mentioned in paragraph (a) or (b) above is in subsections (2) and (5) above referred to as 'relevant property'.

(7) In exercising the powers conferred by this section the court shall have regard to all the circumstances of the case, including any change in any of the matters to which the court was required to have regard when making the order to which the application relates.

(8) Where the court makes an order under this section, it may give such consequential directions as it thinks necessary or expedient having regard to the provisions of the order.

(9) No such order as is mentioned in section 2(1)(d), (e) or (f), 9, 10 or 11 of this Act shall be made on an application under this section.

(10) For the avoidance of doubt it is hereby declared that, in relation to an order which provides for the making of periodical payments which are to cease on the occurrence of an event specified in the order (other than the remarriage of a former wife or former husband) or on the expiration of a period so specified, the power to vary an order includes power to provide for the making of periodical payments after the expiration of that period or the occurrence of that event.

7 Payment of lump sums by instalments

(1) An order under section 2(1)(b) or 6(2)(b) of this Act for the payment of a lump sum may provide for the payment of that sum by instalments of such amount as may be specified in the order.

(2) Where an order is made by virtue of subsection (1) above, the court shall have power, on an application made by the person to whom the lump sum is payable, by the personal representatives of the deceased or by the trustees of the property out of which the lump sum is payable, to vary that order by varying the number of instalments payable, the amount of any instalment and the date on which any instalment becomes payable.

8 Property treated as part of 'net estate'

(1) Where a deceased person has in accordance with the provisions of any enactment nominated any person to receive any sum of money or other property on his death and that nomination is in force at the time of his death, that sum of money, after deducting therefrom any inheritance tax payable in respect thereof, or that other property, to the extent of the value thereof at the date of the death of the deceased after deducting therefrom any inheritance tax so payable, shall be treated for the purposes of this Act as part of the net estate of the deceased; but this subsection shall not render any person liable for having paid that sum or transferred that other property to the person named in the nomination in accordance with the directions given in the nomination.

(2) Where any sum of money or other property is received by any person as a donatio mortis causa made by a deceased person, that sum of money, after deducting therefrom any inheritance tax payable thereon, or that other property, to the extent of the value thereof at the date of the death of the deceased after deducting therefrom any inheritance tax so payable, shall be treated for the

purposes of this Act as part of the net estate of the deceased; but this subsection shall not render any person liable for having paid that sum or transferred that other property in order to give effect to that donatio mortis causa.

(3) The amount of inheritance tax to be deducted for the purposes of this section shall not exceed the amount of that tax which has been borne by the person nominated by the deceased or, as the case may be, the person who has received a sum of money or other property as a donatio mortis causa.

9 Property held on a joint tenancy

(1) Where a deceased person was immediately before his death beneficially entitled to a joint tenancy of any property, then, if, before the end of the period of six months from the date on which representation with respect to the estate of the deceased was first taken out, an application is made for an order under section 2 of this Act, the court for the purpose of facilitating the making of financial provision for the applicant under this Act may order that the deceased's severable share of that property, at the value thereof immediately before his death, shall, to such extent as appears to the court to be just in all the circumstances of the case, be treated for the purposes of this Act as part of the net estate of the deceased.

(2) In determining the extent to which any severable share is to be treated as part of the net estate of the deceased by virtue of an order under subsection (1) above, the court shall have regard to any inheritance tax payable in respect of that severable share.

(3) Where an order is made under subsection (1) above, the provisions of this section shall not render any person liable for anything done by him before the order was made.

(4) For the avoidance of doubt it is hereby declared that for the purposes of this section there may be a joint tenancy of a chose in action.

10 Dispositions intended to defeat applications for financial provision

(1) Where an application is made to the court for an order under section 2 of this Act the applicant may, in the proceedings on that application, apply to the court for an order under subsection (2) below.

(2) Where on an application under subsection (1) above the court is satisfied –

(a) that, less than six years before the date of the death of the deceased, the deceased with the intention of defeating an application for financial provision under this Act made a disposition, and

(b) that full valuable consideration for that disposition was not given by the person to whom or for the benefit of whom the disposition was made (in this section referred to as 'the donee') or by any other person, and

(c) that the exercise of the powers conferred by this section would facilitate the making of financial provision for the applicant under this Act,

then, subject to the provisions of this section and of sections 12 and 13 of this Act, the court may order the donee (whether or not at the date of the order he holds any interest in the property disposed of to him or for his benefit by the deceased) to provide, for the purpose of the making of that financial provision, such sum of money or other property as may be specified in the order.

(3) Where an order is made under subsection (2) above as respects any disposition made by the deceased which consisted of the payment of money to or for the benefit of the donee, the amount of any sum of money or the value of any property ordered to be provided under that subsection shall not exceed the amount of the payment made by the deceased after deducting therefrom any inheritance tax borne by the donee in respect of that payment.

(4) Where an order is made under subsection (2) above as respects any disposition made by the deceased which consisted of the transfer of property (other than a sum of money) to or for the benefit of the donee, the amount of any sum of money or the value of any property ordered to be provided under that subsection shall not exceed the value at the date of the death of the deceased of the property disposed of by him to or for the benefit of the donee (or if that property has been disposed of by the person to whom it was transferred by the deceased, the value at the date of that disposal thereof) after deducting therefrom any inheritance tax borne by the donee in respect of the transfer of that property by the deceased.

(5) Where an application (in this subsection referred to as 'the original application') is made for an order under subsection (2) above in relation to any disposition, then, if on an application under this

subsection by the donee or by any applicant for an order under section 2 of this Act the court is satisfied –

(a) that, less than six years before the date of the death of the deceased, the deceased with the intention of defeating an application for financial provision under this Act made a disposition other than the disposition which is the subject of the original application, and

(b) that full valuable consideration for that other disposition was not given by the person to whom or for the benefit of whom that other disposition was made or by any other person,

the court may exercise in relation to the person to whom or for the benefit of whom that other disposition was made the powers which the court would have had under subsection (2) above if the original application had been made in respect of that other disposition and the court had been satisfied as to the matters set out in paragraphs (a), (b) and (c) of that subsection; and where any application is made under this subsection, any reference in this section (except in subsection (2)(b)) to the donee shall include a reference to the person to whom or for the benefit of whom that other disposition was made.

(6) In determining whether and in what manner to exercise its powers under this section, the court shall have regard to the circumstances in which any disposition was made and any valuable consideration which was given therefor, the relationship, if any, of the donee to the deceased, the conduct and financial resources of the donee and all the other circumstances of the case.

(7) In this section 'disposition' does not include –

(a) any provision in a will, any such nomination as is mentioned in section 8(1) of this Act or any donatio mortis causa, or

(b) any appointment of property made, otherwise than by will, in the exercise of a special power of appointment,

but, subject to these exceptions, includes any payment of money (including the payment of a premium under a policy of assurance) and any conveyance, assurance, appointment or gift of property of any description, whether made by an instrument or otherwise.

(8) The provisions of this section do not apply to any disposition made before the commencement of this Act.

11 Contracts to leave property by will

(1) Where an application is made to a court for an order under section 2 of this Act, the applicant may, in the proceedings on that application, apply to the court for an order under this section.

(2) Where on an application under subsection (1) above the court is satisfied –

(a) that the deceased made a contract by which he agreed to leave by his will a sum of money or other property to any person or by which he agreed that a sum of money or other property would be paid or transferred to any person out of his estate, and

(b) that the deceased made that contract with the intention of defeating an application for financial provision under this Act, and

(c) that when the contract was made full valuable consideration for that contract was not given or promised by the person with whom or for the benefit of whom the contract was made (in this section referred to as 'the donee') or by any other person, and

(d) that the exercise of the powers conferred by this section would facilitate the making of financial provision for the applicant under this Act,

then, subject to the provisions of this section and of sections 12 and 13 of this Act, the court may make any one or more of the following orders, that is to say –

(i) if any money has been paid or any other property has been transferred to or for the benefit of the donee in accordance with the contract, an order directing the donee to provide, for the purpose of the making of that financial provision, such sum of money or other property as may be specified in the order;

(ii) if the money or all the money has not been paid or the property or all the property has not been transferred in accordance with the contract, an order directing the personal representatives not to make any payment or transfer any property, or not to make any further payment or transfer any further property, as the case may be, in accordance therewith or directing the personal representatives only to make such payment or transfer such property as may be specified in the order.

(3) Notwithstanding anything in subsection (2) above, the court may exercise its powers thereunder in relation to any contract made

by the deceased only to the extent that the court considers that the amount of any sum of money paid or to be paid or the value of any property transferred or to be transferred in accordance with the contract exceeds the value of any valuable consideration given or to be given for that contract, and for this purpose the court shall have regard to the value of property at the date of the hearing.

(4) In determining whether and in what manner to exercise its powers under this section, the court shall have regard to the circumstances in which the contract was made, the relationship, if any, of the donee to the deceased, the conduct and financial resources of the donee and all the other circumstances of the case.

(5) Where an order has been made under subsection (2) above in relation to any contract, the rights of any person to enforce that contract or to recover damages or to obtain other relief for the breach thereof shall be subject to any adjustment made by the court under section 12(3) of this Act and shall survive to such extent only as is consistent with giving effect to the terms of that order.

(6) The provisions of this section do not apply to a contract made before the commencement of this Act.

12   Provisions supplementary to ss10 and 11

(1) Where the exercise of any of the powers conferred by section 10 or 11 of this Act is conditional on the court being satisfied that a disposition or contract was made by a deceased person with the intention of defeating an application for financial provision under this Act, that condition shall be fulfilled if the court is of the opinion that, on a balance of probabilities, the intention of the deceased (though not necessarily his sole intention) in making the disposition or contract was to prevent an order for financial provision being made under this Act or to reduce the amount of the provision which might otherwise be granted by an order thereunder.

(2) Where an application is made under section 11 of this Act with respect to any contract made by the deceased and no valuable consideration was given or promised by any person for that contract then, notwithstanding anything in subsection (1) above, it shall be presumed, unless the contrary is shown, that the deceased made that contract with the intention of defeating an application for financial provision under this Act.

(3) Where the court makes an order under section 10 or 11 of this Act it may give such consequential directions as it thinks fit (including directions requiring the making of any payment or the transfer of any property) for giving effect to the order or for securing a fair adjustment of the rights of the persons affected thereby.

(4) Any power conferred on the court by the said section 10 or 11 to order the donee, in relation to any disposition or contract, to provide any sum of money or other property shall be exercisable in like manner in relation to the personal representative of the donee, and –

(a) any reference in section 10(4) to the disposal of property by the donee shall include a reference to disposal by the personal representative of the donee, and

(b) any reference in section 10(5) to an application by the donee under that subsection shall include a reference to an application by the personal representative of the donee;

but the court shall not have power under the said section 10 or 11 to make an order in respect of any property forming part of the estate of the donee which has been distributed by the personal representative; and the personal representative shall not be liable for having distributed any such property before he has notice of the making of an application under the said section 10 or 11 on the ground that he ought to have taken into account the possibility that such an application would be made.

13   Provisions as to trustees in relation to ss10 and 11

(1) Where an application is made for –

(a) an order under section 10 of this Act in respect of a disposition made by the deceased to any person as a trustee, or

(b) an order under section 11 of this Act in respect of any payment made or property transferred, in accordance with a contract made by the deceased, to any person as a trustee,

the powers of the court under the said section 10 or 11 to order that trustee to provide a sum of money or other property shall be subject to the following limitation (in addition, in a case of an application under section 10, to any provision regarding the deduction of inheritance tax) namely, that the amount of any sum of money or the value of any property ordered to be provided –

(i) in the case of an application in respect of a disposition which consisted of the payment of money or an application in respect of the payment of money in accordance with a contract, shall not exceed the aggregate of so much of that money as is at the date of the order in the hands of the trustee and the value at that date of any property which represents that money or is derived therefrom and is at that date in the hands of the trustee;

(ii) in the case of an application in respect of a disposition which consisted of the transfer of property (other than a sum of money) or an application in respect of the transfer of property (other than a sum of money) in accordance with a contract, shall not exceed the aggregate of the value at the date of the order of so much of that property as is at that date in the hands of the trustee and the value at that date of any property which represents the first mentioned property or is derived therefrom and is at that date in the hands of the trustee.

(2) Where any such application is made in respect of a disposition made to any person as a trustee or in respect of any payment made or property transferred in pursuance of a contract to any person as a trustee, the trustee shall not be liable for having distributed any money or other property on the ground that he ought to have taken into account the possibility that such an application would be made.

(3) Where any such application is made in respect of a disposition made to any person as a trustee or in respect of any payment made or property transferred in accordance with a contract to any person as a trustee, any reference in the said section 10 or 11 to the donee shall be construed as including a reference to the trustee or trustees for the time being of the trust in question and any reference in subsection (1) or (2) above to a trustee shall be construed in the same way.

14 Provision as to cases where no financial relief was granted in divorce proceedings, etc

(1) Where, within twelve months from the date on which a decree of divorce or nullity of marriage has been made absolute or a decree of judicial separation has been granted, a party to the marriage dies and –

(a) an application for a financial provision order under section 23 of the Matrimonial Causes Act 1973 or a property adjustment order under section 24 of that Act has not been made by the other party to that marriage, or

(b) such an application has been made but the proceedings thereon have not been determined at the time of the death of the deceased,

then, if an application for an order under section 2 of this Act is made by that other party, the court shall, notwithstanding anything in section 1 or section 3 of this Act, have power, if it thinks it just to do so, to treat that party for the purposes of that application as if the decree of divorce or nullity of marriage had not been made absolute or the decree of judicial separation had not been granted, as the case may be.

(2) This section shall not apply in relation to a decree of judicial separation unless at the date of the death of the deceased the decree was in force and the separation was continuing.

15 Restriction imposed in divorce proceedings, etc on application under this Act

(1) On the grant of a decree of divorce, a decree of nullity of marriage or a decree of judicial separation or at any time thereafter the court, if it considers it just to do so, may, on the application of either party to the marriage, order that the other party to the marriage shall not on the death of the applicant be entitled to apply for an order under section 2 of this Act.

In this subsection 'the court' means the High Court or, where a county court has jurisdiction by virtue of Part V of the Matrimonial and Family Proceedings Act 1984, a county court.

(2) In the case of a decree of divorce or nullity of marriage an order may be made under subsection (1) above before or after the decree is made absolute, but if it is made before the decree is made absolute it shall not take effect unless the decree is made absolute.

(3) Where an order made under subsection (1) above on the grant of a decree of divorce or nullity of marriage has come into force with respect to a party to a marriage, then, on the death of the other party to that marriage, the court shall not entertain any application for an order under section 2 of this Act made by the first-mentioned party.

(4) Where an order made under subsection (1) above on the grant of a decree of judicial separation has come into force with respect to any party to a marriage, then, if the other party to that marriage

dies while the decree is in force and the separation is continuing, the court shall not entertain any application for an order under section 2 of this Act made by the first-mentioned party.

19   Effect, duration and form of orders

(1) Where an order is made under section 2 of this Act then for all purposes, including the purposes of the enactments relating to inheritance tax, the will or the law relating to intestacy, or both the will and the law relating to intestacy, as the case may be, shall have effect and be deemed to have had effect as from the deceased's death subject to the provisions of the order.

(2) Any order made under section 2 or 5 of this Act in favour of –

(a) an applicant who was the former husband or former wife of the deceased, or

(b) an applicant who was the husband or wife of the deceased in a case where the marriage with the deceased was the subject of a decree of judicial separation and at the date of death the decree was in force and the separation was continuing,

shall, in so far as it provides for the making of periodical payments, cease to have effect on the remarriage of the applicant, except in relation to any arrears due under the order on the date of the remarriage.

(3) A copy of every order made under this Act, other than an order made under section 15(1) of this Act, shall be sent to the principal registry of the Family Division for entry and filing, and a memorandum of the order shall be endorsed on, or permanently annexed to, the probate or letters of administration under which the estate is being administered.

20   Provisions as to personal representatives

(1) The provisions of this Act shall not render the personal representative of a deceased person liable for having distributed any part of the estate of the deceased, after the end of the period of six months from the date on which representation with respect to the estate of the deceased is first taken out, on the ground that he ought to have taken into account the possibility –

(a) that the court might permit the making of an application for an order under section 2 of this Act after the end of that period, or

(b) that, where an order has been made under the said section 2, the court might exercise in relation thereto the powers conferred on it by section 6 of this Act,

but this subsection shall not prejudice any power to recover, by reason of the making of an order under this Act, any part of the estate so distributed.

(2) Where the personal representative of a deceased person pays any sum directed by an order under section 5 of this Act to be paid out of the deceased's net estate, he shall not be under any liability by reason of that estate not being sufficient to make the payment, unless at the time of making the payment he has reasonable cause to believe that the estate is not sufficient.

(3) Where a deceased person entered into a contract by which he agreed to leave by his will any sum of money or other property to any person or by which he agreed that a sum of money or other property would be paid or transferred to any person out of his estate, then, if the personal representative of the deceased has reason to believe that the deceased entered into the contract with the intention of defeating an application for financial provision under this Act, he may, notwithstanding anything in that contract, postpone the payment of that sum of money or the transfer of that property until the expiration of the period of six months from the date on which representation with respect to the estate of the deceased is first taken out or, if during that period an application is made for an order under section 2 of this Act, until the determination of the proceedings on that application.

21 Admissibility as evidence of statements made by deceased

In any proceedings under this Act a statement made by the deceased, whether orally or in a document or otherwise, shall be admissible under section 2 of the Civil Evidence Act 1968 as evidence of any fact stated therein in like manner as if the statement were a statement falling within section 2(1) of that Act; and any reference in that Act to a statement admissible, or given or proposed to be given, in evidence under section 2 thereof or to the admissibility or the giving in evidence of a statement by virtue of that section or to any statement falling within section 2(1) of that Act shall be construed accordingly.

23 Determination of date on which representation was first taken out

In considering for the purposes of this Act when representation with respect to the estate of a deceased person was first taken out, a grant limited to settled land or to trust property shall be left out of account, and a grant limited to real estate or to personal estate shall be left out of account unless a grant limited to the remainder of the estate has previously been made or is made at the same time.

24 Effect of this Act on s46(1)(vi) of Administration of Estates Act 1925

Section 46(1)(vi) of the Administration of Estates Act 1925, in so far as it provides for the devolution of property on the Crown, the Duchy of Lancaster or the Duke of Cornwall as bona vacantia, shall have effect subject to the provisions of this Act.

25 Interpretation

(1) In this Act –

'beneficiary', in relation to the estate of a deceased person, means –

(a) a person who under the will of the deceased or under the law relating to intestacy is beneficially interested in the estate or would be so interested if an order had not been made under this Act, and

(b) a person who has received any sum of money or other property which by virtue of section 8(1) or 8(2) of this Act is treated as part of the net estate of the deceased or would have received that sum or other property if an order had not been made under this Act;

'child' includes an illegitimate child and a child en ventre sa mere at the death of the deceased;

'the court', unless the context otherwise requires, means the High Court, or where a county court has jurisdiction by virtue of section 22 of this Act, a county court;

'former wife' or 'former husband' means a person whose marriage with the deceased was during the lifetime of the deceased either –

(a) dissolved or annulled by a decree of divorce or a decree of nullity of marriage granted under the law of any part of the British Islands, or

(b) dissolved or annulled in any country or territory outside the British Islands by a divorce or annulment which is entitled to be recognised as valid by the law of England and Wales;

'net estate', in relation to a deceased person, means –

(a) all property of which the deceased had power to dispose by his will (otherwise than by virtue of a special power of appointment) less the amount of his funeral, testamentary and administration expenses, debts and liabilities, including any inheritance tax payable out of his estate on his death;

(b) any property in respect of which the deceased held a general power of appointment (not being a power exercisable by will) which has not been exercised;

(c) any sum of money or other property which is treated for the purposes of this Act as part of the net estate of the deceased by virtue of section 8(1) or (2) of this Act;

(d) any property which is treated for the purposes of this Act as part of the net estate of the deceased by virtue of an order made under section 9 of this Act;

(e) any sum of money or other property which is, by reason of a disposition or contract made by the deceased, ordered under section 10 or 11 of this Act to be provided for the purpose of the making of financial provision under this Act;

'property' includes any chose in action;

'reasonable financial provision' has the meaning assigned to it by section 1 of this Act;

'valuable consideration' does not include marriage or a promise of marriage;

'will' includes codicil.

(2) For the purposes of paragraph (a) of the definition of 'net estate' in subsection (1) above a person who is not of full age and capacity shall be treated as having power to dispose by will of all property of which he would have had power to dispose by will if he had been of full age and capacity.

(3) Any reference in this Act to provision out of the net estate of a deceased person includes a reference to provision extending to the whole of that estate.

(4) For the purposes of this Act any reference to a wife or husband shall be treated as including a reference to a person who in good faith entered into a void marriage with the deceased unless either –

(a) the marriage of the deceased and that person was dissolved or annulled during the lifetime of the deceased and the dissolution or annulment is recognised by the law of England and Wales, or

(b) that person has during the lifetime of the deceased entered into a later marriage.

(5) Any reference in this Act to remarriage or to a person who has remarried includes a reference to a marriage which is by law void or voidable or to a person who has entered into such a marriage, as the case may be, and a marriage shall be treated for the purposes of this Act as a remarriage, in relation to any party thereto, notwithstanding that the previous marriage of that party was void or voidable.

(6) Any reference in this Act to an order or decree made under the Matrimonial Causes Act 1973 or under any section of that Act shall be construed as including a reference to an order or decree which is deemed to have been made under that Act or under that section thereof, as the case may be.

(7) Any reference in this Act to any enactment is a reference to that enactment as amended by or under any subsequent enactment.

As amended by the Administration of Justice Act 1982, s52; Matrimonial and Family Proceedings Act 1984, ss8, 25(2).

LEGITIMACY ACT 1976
(1976 c 31)

1   Legitimacy of children in certain void marriages

(1) The child of a void marriage, whenever born, shall, subject to subsection (2) below and Schedule 1 to this Act, be treated as the legitimate child of his parents if at the time of the insemination resulting in the birth or, where there was no such insemination, the child's conception (or at the time of the celebration of the marriage if later) both or either of the parties reasonably believed that the marriage was valid.

(2) This section only applies where the father of the child was domiciled in England and Wales at the time of the birth or, if he died before the birth, was so domiciled immediately before his death.

(3) It is hereby declared for the avoidance of doubt that subsection (1) above applies notwithstanding that the belief that the marriage was valid was due to a mistake as to law ...

2   Legitimation by subsequent marriage of parents

Subject to the following provisions of this Act, where the parents of an illegitimate person marry one another, the marriage shall, if the father of the illegitimate person is at the date of marriage domiciled in England and Wales, render that person, if living, legitimate from the date of the marriage.

3   Legitimation by extraneous law

Subject to the following provisions of this Act, where the parents of an illegitimate person marry one another and the father of the illegitimate person is not at the time of the marriage domiciled in England and Wales but is domiciled in a country by the law of which the illegitimate person became legitimated by virtue of such subsequent marriage, that person, if living, shall in England and

Wales be recognised as having been so legitimated from the date of the marriage notwithstanding that, at the time of his birth, his father was domiciled in a country the law of which did not permit legitimation by subsequent marriage.

4 Legitimation of adopted child

(1) Section 39 of the Adoption Act 1976 does not prevent an adopted child being legitimated under section 2 or 3 above if either natural parent is the sole adoptive parent.

(2) Where an adopted child (with a sole adoptive parent) is legitimated –

(a) subsection (2) of the said section 39 shall not apply after the legitimation to the natural relationship with the other natural parent, and

(b) revocation of the adoption order in consequence of the legitimation shall not affect section 39, 41 or 42 of the Adoption Act 1976 as it applies to any instrument made before the date of legitimation.

5 Rights of legitimated persons and others to take interests in property

(1) Subject to any contrary indication, the rules of construction contained in this section apply to any instrument other than an existing instrument, so far as the instrument contains a disposition of property.

(2) For the purposes of this section, provisions of the law of intestate succession applicable to the estate of a deceased person shall be treated as if contained in an instrument executed by him (while of full capacity) immediately before his death.

(3) A legitimated person, and any other person, shall be entitled to take any interest as if the legitimated person had been born legitimate.

(4) A disposition which depends on the date of birth of a child or children of the parent or parents shall be construed as if –

(a) a legitimated child had been born on the date of legitimation,

(b) two or more legitimated children legitimated on the same date had been born on that date in the order of their actual births,

but this does not affect any reference to the age of a child.

(5) Examples of phrases in wills on which subsection (4) above can operate are –

1. Children of A 'living at my death or born afterwards'.

2. Children of A 'living at my death or born afterwards before any one of such children for the time being in existence attains a vested interest, and who attain the age of 21 years'.

3. As in example 1 or 2, but referring to grandchildren of A, instead of children of A.

4. A for life 'until he has a child' and then to his child or children.

Note. Subsection (4) above will not affect the reference to the age of 21 years in example 2.

(6) If an illegitimate person or a person adopted by one of his natural parents dies, or has died before the commencement of this Act, and –

(a) after his death his parents marry or have married; and

(b) the deceased would, if living at the time of the marriage, have become a legitimated person,

this section shall apply for the construction of the instrument so far as it relates to the taking of interests by, or in succession to, his spouse, children and remoter issue as if he had been legitimated by virtue of the marriage.

(7) In this section 'instrument' includes a private Act settling property, but not any other enactment.

6   Dispositions depending on date of birth

(1) Where a disposition depends on the date of birth of a child who was born illegitimate and who is legitimated (or, if deceased, is treated as legitimated), section 5(4) above does not affect entitlement under Part II of the Family Law Reform Act 1969 (illegitimate children).

(2) Where a disposition depends on the date of birth of an adopted child who is legitimated (or, if deceased, is treated as legitimated)

section 5(4) above does not affect entitlement by virtue of section 42(2) of the Adoption Act 1976.

(3) This section applies for example where –

(a) a testator dies in 1976 bequeathing a legacy to his eldest grandchild living at a specified time,

(b) a daughter has an illegitimate child in 1977 who is the first grandchild,

(c) his married son has a child in 1978,

(d) subsequently the illegitimate child is legitimated,

and in all those cases the daughter's child remains the eldest grandchild of the testator throughout.

7   Protection of trustees and personal representatives

(1) A trustee or personal representative is not under a duty, by virtue of the law relating to trusts or the administration of estates, to enquire, before conveying or distributing any property, whether any person is illegitimate or has been adopted by one of his natural parents, and could be legitimated (or if deceased be treated as legitimated), if that fact could affect entitlement to the property.

(2) A trustee or personal representative shall not be liable to any person by reason of a conveyance or distribution of the property made without regard to any such fact if he has not received notice of the fact before the conveyance or distribution.

(3) This section does not prejudice the right of a person to follow the property, or any property representing it, into the hands of another person, other than a purchaser, who has received it.

10   Interpretation

(1) In this Act, except where the context otherwise requires, –

'disposition' includes the conferring of a power of appointment and any other disposition of an interest in or right over property;

'existing', in relation to an instrument, means one made before 1 January 1976;

'legitimated person' means a person legitimated or recognised as legitimated –

(a) under section 2 or 3 above; or

(b) under section 1 or 8 of the Legitimacy Act 1926; or

(c) except in section 8, by a legitimation (whether or not by virtue of the subsequent marriage of his parents) recognised by the law of England and Wales and effected under the law of any other country;

and cognate expressions shall be construed accordingly;

'power of appointment' includes any discretionary power to transfer a beneficial interest in property without the furnishing of valuable consideration;

'void marriage' means a marriage, not being voidable only, in respect of which the High Court has or had jurisdiction to grant a decree of nullity, or would have or would have had such jurisdiction if the parties were domiciled in England and Wales ...

(3) For the purpose of this Act, except where the context otherwise requires, –

(a) the death of the testator is the date at which a will or codicil is to be regarded as made;

(b) an oral disposition of property shall be deemed to be contained in an instrument made when the disposition was made.

(4) It is hereby declared that references in this Act to dispositions of property include references to a disposition by the creation of an entailed interest.

As amended by the Adoption Act 1976, s73(2), Schedule 3, paras 23, 24; Family Law Reform Act 1987, s28.

ADOPTION ACT 1976
(1976 c 36)

39 Status conferred by adoption

(1) An adopted child shall be treated in law –

(a) where the adopters are a married couple, as if he had been born as a child of the marriage (whether or not he was in fact born after the marriage was solemnised);

(b) in any other case, as if he had been born to the adopter in wedlock (but not as a child of any actual marriage of the adopter).

(2) An adopted child shall, subject to subsection (3), be treated in law as if he were not the child of any person other than the adopters or adopter.

(3) In the case of a child adopted by one of its natural parents as sole adoptive parent, subsection (2) has no effect as respects entitlement to property depending on relationship to that parent, or as respects anything else depending on that relationship.

(4) It is hereby declared that this section prevents an adopted child from being illegitimate.

(5) This section has effect –

(a) in the case of an adoption before 1 January 1976, from that date, and

(b) in the case of any other adoption, from the date of the adoption.

(6) Subject to the provisions of this Part, this section –

(a) applies for the construction of enactments or instruments passed or made before the adoption or later, and so applies subject to any contrary indication; and

(b) has effect as respects things done, or events occurring, after the adoption, or after 31 December 1975, whichever is the later.

41 Adoptive relatives

(1) A relationship existing by virtue of section 39 may be referred to as an adoptive relationship, and –

(a) a male adopter may be referred to as the adoptive father;

(b) a female adopter may be referred to as the adoptive mother;

(c) any other relative of any degree under an adoptive relationship may be referred to as an adoptive relative of that degree,

but this section does not prevent the term 'parent', or any other term not qualified by the word 'adoptive', being treated as including an adoptive relative.

42 Rules of construction for instruments concerning property

(1) Subject to any contrary indication, the rules of construction contained in this section apply to any instrument, other than an existing instrument, so far as it contains a disposition of property.

(2) In applying section 39(1) to a disposition which depends on the date of birth of a child or children of the adoptive parent or parents, the disposition shall be construed as if –

(a) the adopted child had been born on the date of adoption,

(b) two or more children adopted on the same date had been born on that date in the order of their actual births,

but this does not affect any reference to the age of a child.

(3) Examples of phrases in wills on which subsection (2) can operate are –

1. Children of A 'living at my death or born afterwards'.

2. Children of A 'living at my death or born afterwards before any one of such children for the time being in existence attains a vested interest and who attain the age of 21 years'.

3. As in example 1 or 2, but referring to grandchildren of A instead of children of A.

4. A for life 'until he has a child', and then to his child or children.

Note. Subsection (2) will not affect the reference to the age of 21 years in example 2.

(4) Section 39(2) does not prejudice any interest vested in possession in the adopted child before the adoption, or any interest expectant (whether immediately or not) upon an interest so vested.

(5) Where it is necessary to determine for the purposes of a disposition of property effected by an instrument whether a woman can have a child, it shall be presumed that once a woman has attained the age of 55 years she will not adopt a child after execution of the instrument, and, notwithstanding section 39, if she does so that child shall not be treated as her child or as the child of her spouse (if any) for the purposes of the instrument.

(6) In this section, 'instrument' includes a private Act settling property, but not any other enactment.

45   Protection of trustees and personal representatives

(1) A trustee or personal representative is not under a duty, by virtue of the law relating to trusts or the administration of estates, to enquire, before conveying or distributing any property, whether any adoption has been effected or revoked if that fact could affect entitlement to the property.

(2) A trustee or personal representative shall not be liable to any person by reason of a conveyance or distribution of the property made without regard to any such fact if he has not received notice of the fact before the conveyance or distribution.

(3) This section does not prejudice the right of a person to follow the property, or any property representing it, into the hands of another person, other than a purchaser, who has received it.

46   Meaning of 'disposition'

(1) In this Part, unless the context otherwise requires, –

'disposition' includes the conferring of a power of appointment and any other disposition of an interest in or right over property;

'power of appointment' includes any discretionary power to transfer a beneficial interest in property without the furnishing of valuable consideration.

(2) This Part applies to an oral disposition as if contained in an instrument made when the disposition was made.

(3) For the purposes of this Part, the death of the testator is the date at which a will or codicil is to be regarded as made.

(4) For the purposes of this Part, provisions of the law of intestate succession applicable to the estate of a deceased person shall be treated as if contained in an instrument executed by him (while of full capacity) immediately before his death.

(5) It is hereby declared that references in this Part to dispositions of property include references to a disposition by the creation of an entailed interest.

INTERPRETATION ACT 1978
(1978 c 30)

5   Definitions

In any Act, unless the contrary intention appears, words and expressions listed in Schedule 1 to this Act are to be construed according to that Schedule.

6   Gender and number

In any Act, unless the contrary intention appears, –

(a) words importing the masculine gender include the feminine;

(b) words importing the feminine gender include the masculine;

(c) words in the singular include the plural and words in the plural include the singular.

SCHEDULE 1

WORDS AND EXPRESSIONS DEFINED ...

In relation to England and Wales –

(a) references (however expressed) to any relationship between two persons;

(b) references to a person whose father and mother were or were not married to each other at the time of his birth; and

(c) references cognate with references falling within paragraph (b) above,

shall be construed in accordance with section 1 of the Family Law Reform Act 1987.

LIMITATION ACT 1980
(1980 c 58)

15 Time limit for actions to recover land

(1) No action shall be brought by any person to recover any land after the expiration of twelve years from the date on which the right of action accrued to him or, if it first accrued to some person through whom he claims, to that person ...

(6) Part I of Schedule 1 to this Act contains provisions for determining the date of accrual of rights of action to recover land in the cases there mentioned ...

21 Time limit for actions in respect of trust property

(1) No period of limitation prescribed by this Act shall apply to an action by a beneficiary under a trust, being an action –

(a) in respect of any fraud or fraudulent breach of trust to which the trustee was a party or privy; or

(b) to recover from the trustee trust property or the proceeds of trust property in the possession of the trustee, or previously received by the trustee and converted to his use.

(2) Where a trustee who is also a beneficiary under the trust received or retains trust property or its proceeds as his share on a distribution of trust property under the trust, his liability in any action brought by virtue of subsection (1)(b) above to recover that property or its proceeds after the expiration of the period of limitation prescribed by this Act for bringing an action to recover trust property shall be limited to the excess over his proper share.

This subsection only applies if the trustee acted honestly and reasonably in making the distribution.

(3) Subject to the preceding provisions of this section, an action by a beneficiary to recover trust property or in respect of any breach

of trust, not being an action for which a period of limitation is prescribed by any other provision of this Act, shall not be brought after the expiration of six years from the date on which the right of action accrued.

For the purposes of this subsection, the right of action shall not be treated as having accrued to any beneficiary entitled to a future interest in the trust property until the interest fell into possession.

(4) No beneficiary as against whom there would be a good defence under this Act shall derive any greater or other benefit from a judgment or order obtained by any other beneficiary than he could have obtained if he had brought the action and this Act had been pleaded in defence.

22 Time limit for actions claiming personal estate of a deceased person

Subject to section 21(1) and (2) of this Act –

(a) no action in respect of any claim to the personal estate of a deceased person or to any share or interest in any such estate (whether under a will or on intestacy) shall be brought after the expiration of twelve years from the date on which the right to receive the share or interest accrued; and

(b) no action to recover arrears of interest in respect of any legacy, or damages in respect of such arrears, shall be brought after the expiration of six years from the date on which the interest became due.

SCHEDULE 1

PROVISIONS WITH RESPECT TO ACTIONS TO RECOVER LAND

PART I

ACCRUAL OF RIGHTS OF ACTION TO RECOVER LAND

2. Where any person brings an action to recover any land of a deceased person (whether under a will or on intestacy) and the deceased person –

(a) was on the date of his death in possession of the land or, in the case of a rentcharge created by will or taking effect upon his death, in possession of the land charged; and

(b) was the last person entitled to the land to be in possession of it;

the right of action shall be treated as having accrued on the date of his death.

SUPREME COURT ACT 1981
(1981 c 54)

61 Distribution of business among Divisions

(1) Subject to any provision made by or under this or any other Act (and in particular to any rules of court made in pursuance of subsection (2) and any order under subsection (3)), business in the High Court of any description mentioned in Schedule 1, as for the time being in force, shall be distributed among the Divisions in accordance with that Schedule.

PART V

PROBATE CAUSES AND MATTERS

105 Applications

Applications for grants of probate or administration and for the revocation of grants may be made to –

   (a) the Principal Registry of the Family Division (in this Part referred to as 'the Principal Registry'); or

   (b) a district probate registry.

106 Grants by district probate registrars

(1) Any grant made by a district probate registrar shall be made in the name of the High Court under the seal used in the registry.

107 No grant where conflicting applications

Subject to probate rules, no grant in respect of the estate, or part of the estate, of a deceased person shall be made out of the Principal Registry or any district probate registry on any application if, at any time before the making of a grant, it appears to the registrar concerned that some other application has been made in respect of that estate or, as the case may be, that part of it and has not been either refused or withdrawn.

108 Caveats

(1) A caveat against a grant of probate or administration may be entered in the Principal Registry or in any district probate registry.

(2) On a caveat being entered in a district probate registry, the district probate registrar shall immediately send a copy of it to the Principal Registry to be entered among the caveats in that Registry.

109 Refusal of grant where capital transfer tax unpaid

(1) Subject to subsections (2) and (3), no grant shall be made, and no grant made outside the United Kingdom shall be resealed, except on the production of an account prepared in pursuance of the Inheritance Tax Act 1984 showing by means of such receipt or certification as may be prescribed by the Commissioners of Inland Revenue (in this and the following section referred to as 'the Commissioners') either –

(a) that the inheritance tax payable on the delivery of the account has been paid; or

(b) that no such tax is so payable.

(2) Arrangements may be made between the President of the Family Division and the Commissioners providing for the purposes of this section in such cases as may be specified in the arrangements that the receipt or certification of an account may be dispensed with or that some other document may be substituted for the account required by the Inheritance Tax Act 1984.

(3) Nothing in subsection (1) applies in relation to a case where the delivery of the account required by that Part of that Act has for the time being been dispensed with by any regulations under section 256(1)(a) of the Inheritance Tax Act 1984.

111 Records of grants

(1) There shall continue to be kept records of all grants which are made in the Principal Registry or in any district probate registry.

(2) Those records shall be in such form, and shall contain such particulars, as the President of the Family Division may direct.

112 Summons to executor to prove or renounce

The High Court may summon any person named as executor in a will to prove, or renounce probate of, the will, and to do such other things concerning the will as the court had power to order such a person to do immediately before the commencement of this Act.

113 Power of court to sever grant

(1) Subject to subsection (2), the High Court may grant probate or administration in respect of any part of the estate of a deceased person, limited in any way the court thinks fit.

(2) Where the estate of a deceased person is known to be insolvent, the grant of representation to it shall not be severed under subsection (1) except as regards a trust estate in which he had no beneficial interest.

114 Number of personal representatives

(1) Probate or administration shall not be granted by the High Court to more than four persons in respect of the same part of the estate of a deceased person.

(2) Where under a will or intestacy any beneficiary is a minor or a life interest arises, any grant of administration by the High Court shall be made either to a trust corporation (with or without an individual) or to not less than two individuals, unless it appears to the court to be expedient in all the circumstances to appoint an individual as sole administrator.

(3) For the purpose of determining whether a minority or life interest arises in any particular case, the court may act on such evidence as may be prescribed.

(4) If at any time during the minority of a beneficiary or the subsistence of a life interest under a will or intestacy there is only one personal representative (not being a trust corporation), the High Court may, on the application of any person interested or the guardian or receiver of any such person, and in accordance with

probate rules, appoint one or more additional personal representatives to act while the minority or life interest subsists and until the estate is fully administered.

(5) An appointment of an additional personal representative under subsection (4) to act with an executor shall not have the effect of including him in any chain of representation.

115 Grants to trust corporations

(1) The High Court may –

(a) where a trust corporation is named in a will as executor, grant probate to the corporation either solely or jointly with any other person named in the will as executor, as the case may require; or

(b) grant administration to a trust corporation, either solely or jointly with another person;

and the corporation may act accordingly as executor or administrator, as the case may be.

(2) Probate or administration shall not be granted to any person as nominee of a trust corporation.

(3) Any officer authorised for the purpose by a trust corporation or its directors or governing body may, on behalf of the corporation, swear affidavits, give security and do any other act which the court may require with a view to the grant to the corporation of probate or administration; and the acts of an officer so authorised shall be binding on the corporation.

116 Power of court to pass over prior claims to grant

(1) If by reason of any special circumstances it appears to the High Court to be necessary or expedient to appoint as administrator some person other than the person who, but for this section, would in accordance with probate rules have been entitled to the grant, the court may in its discretion appoint as administrator such person as it thinks expedient.

(2) Any grant of administration under this section may be limited in any way the court thinks fit.

117 Administration pending suit

(1) Where any legal proceedings concerning the validity of the will of a deceased person, or for obtaining, recalling or revoking any grant, are pending, the High Court may grant administration of the estate of the deceased person in question to an administrator pending suit, who shall, subject to subsection (2), have all the rights, duties and powers of a general administrator.

(2) An administrator pending suit shall be subject to the immediate control of the court and act under its direction; and, except in such circumstances as may be prescribed, no distribution of the estate, or any part of the estate, of the deceased person in question shall be made by such an administrator without the leave of the court.

(3) The court may, out of the estate of the deceased, assign an administrator pending suit such reasonable remuneration as it thinks fit.

118 Effect of appointment of minor as executor

Where a testator by his will appoints a minor to be an executor, the appointment shall not operate to vest in the minor the estate, or any part of the estate, of the testator, or to constitute him a personal representative for any purpose, unless and until probate is granted to him in accordance with probate rules.

119 Administration with will annexed

(1) Administration with the will annexed shall be granted, subject to and in accordance with probate rules, in every class of case in which the High Court had power to make such a grant immediately before the commencement of this Act.

(2) Where administration with the will annexed is granted, the will of the deceased shall be performed and observed in the same manner as if probate of it had been granted to an executor.

120 Power to require administrators to produce sureties

(1) As a condition of granting administration to any person the High Court may, subject to the following provisions of this section and subject to and in accordance with probate rules, require one or more

sureties to guarantee that they will make good, within any limit imposed by the court on the total liability of the surety or sureties, any loss which any person interested in the administration of the estate of the deceased may suffer in consequence of a breach by the administrator of his duties as such.

(2) A guarantee given in pursuance of any such requirement shall enure for the benefit of every person interested in the administration of the estate of the deceased as if contained in a contract under seal made by the surety or sureties with every such person and, where there are two or more sureties, as if they had bound themselves jointly and severally.

(3) No action shall be brought on any such guarantee without the leave of the High Court.

(4) Stamp duty shall not be chargeable on any such guarantee.

(5) This section does not apply where administration is granted to the Treasury Solicitor, the Official Solicitor, the Public Trustee, the Solicitor for the affairs of the Duchy of Lancaster or the Duchy of Cornwall or the Crown Solicitor for Northern Ireland, or to the consular officer of a foreign state to which section 1 of the Consular Conventions Act 1949 applies, or in such other cases as may be prescribed.

121 Revocation of grants and cancellation of resealing at instance of court

(1) Where it appears to the High Court that a grant either ought not to have been made or contains an error, the court may call in the grant and, if satisfied that it would be revoked at the instance of a party interested, may revoke it.

(2) A grant may be revoked under subsection (1) without being called in, if it cannot be called in.

(3) Where it appears to the High Court that a grant resealed under the Colonial Probates Acts 1892 and 1927 ought not to have been resealed, the court may call in the relevant document and, if satisfied that the resealing would be cancelled at the instance of a party interested, may cancel the resealing.

In this and the following subsection 'the relevant document' means the original grant or, where some other document was sealed by the court under those Acts, the document.

(4) A resealing may be cancelled under subsection (3) without the relevant document being called in, if it cannot be called in.

122 Examination of person with knowledge of testamentary document

(1) Where it appears that there are reasonable grounds for believing that any person has knowledge of any document which is or purports to be a testamentary document, the High Court may, whether or not any legal proceedings are pending, order him to attend for the purpose of being examined in open court.

(2) The court may –

(a) require any person who is before it in compliance with an order under subsection (1) to answer any question relating to the document concerned; and

(b) if appropriate, order him to bring in the document in such manner as the court may direct.

(3) Any person who, having been required by the court to do so under this section, fails to attend for examination, answer any question or bring in any document shall be guilty of contempt of court.

123 Subpoena to bring in testamentary document

Where it appears that any person has in his possession, custody or power any document which is or purports to be a testamentary document, the High Court may, whether or not any legal proceedings are pending, issue a subpoena requiring him to bring in the document in such manner as the court may in the subpoena direct.

124 Place for deposit of original wills and other documents

All original wills and other documents which are under the control of the High Court in the Principal Registry or in any district probate registry shall be deposited and preserved in such places as the Lord Chancellor may direct; and any wills or other documents so deposited shall, subject to the control of the High Court and to probate rules, be open to inspection.

128 Interpretation of Part V and other probate provisions

In this Part, and in the other provisions of this Act relating to probate causes and matters, unless the context otherwise requires –

'administration' includes all letters of administration of the effects of deceased persons, whether with or without a will annexed, and whether granted for general, special or limited purposes;

'estate' means real and personal estate, and 'real estate' includes –

(a) chattels real and land in possession, remainder or reversion and every interest in or over land to which the deceased person was entitled at the time of his death, and

(b) real estate held on trust or by way of mortgage or security, but not money to arise under a trust for sale of land, nor money secured or charged on land;

'grant' means a grant of probate or administration;

'non-contentious or common form probate business' means the business of obtaining probate and administration where there is no contention as to the right thereto, including –

(a) the passing of probates and administration through the High Court in contentious cases where the contest has been terminated,

(b) all business of a non-contentious nature in matters of testacy and intestacy not being proceedings in any action, and

(c) the business of lodging caveats against the grant of probate or administration;

'Principal Registry' means the Principal Registry of the Family Division;

'probate rules' means rules of court made under section 127;

'trust corporation' means the Public Trustee or a corporation either appointed by the court in any particular case to be a trustee or authorised by rules made under section 4(3) of the Public Trustee Act 1906 to act as a custodian trustee;

'will' includes a nuncupative will and any testamentary document of which probate may be granted.

SCHEDULE 1

DISTRIBUTION OF BUSINESS IN HIGH COURT

1. To the Chancery Division are assigned all causes and matters relating to –

(d) the administration of the estates of deceased persons;

(h) probate business, other than non-contentious or common form business.

3. To the Family Division are assigned –

(b) all causes and matters (whether at first instance or on appeal) relating to –

(i) legitimacy;

(iv) non-contentious or common form probate business.

(g) all proceedings for the purpose of enforcing an order made in any proceedings of a type described in this paragraph.

As amended by the Inheritance Tax Act 1984, s276, Schedule 8, para 20; Courts and Legal Services Act 1990, s54(2); High Court (Distribution of Business) Order 1991.

FORFEITURE ACT 1982
(1982 c 34)

1 The 'forfeiture rule'

(1) In this Act, the 'forfeiture rule' means the rule of public policy which in certain circumstances precludes a person who has unlawfully killed another from acquiring a benefit in consequence of the killing.

(2) References in this Act to a person who has unlawfully killed another include a reference to a person who has unlawfully aided, abetted, counselled or procured the death of that other and references in this Act to unlawful killing shall be interpreted accordingly.

2 Power to modify the rule

(1) Where a court determines that the forfeiture rule has precluded a person (in this section referred to as 'the offender') who has unlawfully killed another from acquiring any interest in property mentioned in subsection (4) below, the court may make an order under this section modifying the effect of that rule.

(2) The court shall not make an order under this section modifying the effect of the forfeiture rule in any case unless it is satisfied that, having regard to the conduct of the offender and of the deceased and to such other circumstances as appear to the court to be material, the justice of the case requires the effect of the rule to be so modified in that case.

(3) In any case where a person stands convicted of an offence of which unlawful killing is an element, the court shall not make an order under this section modifying the effect of the forfeiture rule in that case unless proceedings for the purpose are brought before the expiry of the period of three months beginning with his conviction.

(4) The interests in property referred to in subsection (1) above are –

(a) any beneficial interest in property which (apart from the forfeiture rule) the offender would have acquired –

(i) under the deceased's will (including, as respects Scotland, any writing having testamentary effect) or the law relating to intestacy or by way of ius relicti, ius relictae or legitim;

(ii) on the nomination of the deceased in accordance with the provisions of any enactment;

(iii) as a donatio mortis causa made by the deceased; or

(iv) under a special destination (whether relating to heritable or moveable property); or

(b) any beneficial interest in property which (apart from the forfeiture rule) the offender would have acquired in consequence of the death of the deceased, being property which, before the death, was held on trust for any person.

(5) An order under this section may modify the effect of the forfeiture rule in respect of any interest in property to which the determination referred to in subsection (1) above relates and may do so in either or both of the following ways, that is –

(a) where there is more than one such interest, by excluding the application of the rule in respect of any (but not all) of those interests; and

(b) in the case of any such interest in property, by excluding the application of the rule in respect of part of the property.

(6) On the making of an order under this section, the forfeiture rule shall have effect for all purposes (including purposes relating to anything done before the order is made) subject to the modifications made by the order.

(7) The court shall not make an order under this section modifying the effect of the forfeiture rule in respect of any interest in property which, in consequence of the rule, has been acquired before the coming into force of this section by a person other than the offender or a person claiming through him.

(8) In this section –

'property' includes any chose in action or incorporeal moveable property; and

'will' includes codicil.

3 Application for financial provision not affected by the rule

(1) The forfeiture rule shall not be taken to preclude any person from making any application under a provision mentioned in subsection (2) below or the making of any order on the application.

(2) The provisions referred to in subsection (1) above are –

   (a) any provision of the Inheritance (Provision for Family and Dependants) Act 1975 ...

5 Exclusion of murderers

Nothing in this Act or in any order made under section 2 or referred to in section 3(1) of this Act ... shall affect the application of the forfeiture rule in the case of a person who stands convicted of murder.

ADMINISTRATION OF JUSTICE ACT 1982
(1982 c 53)

20 Rectification

(1) If a court is satisfied that a will is so expressed that it fails to carry out the testator's intentions, in consequence –

(a) of a clerical error; or

(b) of a failure to understand his instructions,

it may order that the will shall be rectified so as to carry out his intentions.

(2) An application for an order under this section shall not, except with the permission of the court, be made after the end of the period of six months from the date on which representation with respect to the estate of the deceased is first taken out.

(3) The provisions of this section shall not render the personal representatives of a deceased person liable for having distributed any part of the estate of the deceased, after the end of the period of six months from the date on which representation with respect to the estate of the deceased is first taken out, on the ground that they ought to have taken into account the possibility that the court might permit the making of an application for an order under this section after the end of that period; but this subsection shall not prejudice any power to recover, by reason of the making of an order under this section, any part of the estate so distributed.

(4) In considering for the purposes of this section when representation with respect to the estate of a deceased person was first taken out, a grant limited to settled land or to trust property shall be left out of account, and a grant limited to real estate or to personal estate shall be left out of account unless a grant limited to the remainder of the estate has previously been made or is made at the same time.

21 Interpretation of wills – general rules as to evidence

(1) This section applies to a will –

(a) in so far as any part of it is meaningless;

(b) in so far as the language used in any part of it is ambiguous on the face of it;

(c) in so far as evidence, other than evidence of the testator's intention, shows that the language used in any part of it is ambiguous in the light of surrounding circumstances.

(2) In so far as this section applies to a will extrinsic evidence, including evidence of the testator's intention, may be admitted to assist in its interpretation.

22 Presumption as to effect of gifts to spouses

Except where a contrary intention is shown it shall be presumed that if a testator devises or bequeaths property to his spouse in terms which in themselves would give an absolute interest to the spouse, but by the same instrument purports to give his issue an interest in the same property, the gift to the spouse is absolute notwithstanding the purported gift to the issue.

MENTAL HEALTH ACT 1983
(1983 c 20)

94 Exercise of the judge's functions: 'the patient'

(1) The functions expressed to be conferred by this Part of this Act on the judge shall be exercisable by the Lord Chancellor or by any nominated judge, and shall also be exercisable by the Master of the Court of Protection or by any nominated officer ... and references in this Part of this Act to the judge shall be construed accordingly.

(2) The functions of the judge under this Part of this Act shall be exercisable where, after considering medical evidence, he is satisfied that a person is incapable, by reason of mental disorder, of managing and administering his property and affairs; and a person as to whom the judge is so satisfied is referred to in this Part of this Act as a patient.

95 General functions of the judge with respect to property and affairs of patient

(1) The judge may, with respect to the property and affairs of a patient, do or secure the doing of all such things as appear necessary or expedient –

(a) for the maintenance or other benefit of the patient,

(b) for the maintenance or other benefit of members of the patient's family,

(c) for making provision for other persons or purposes for whom or which the patient might be expected to provide if he were not mentally disordered, or

(d) otherwise for administering the patient's affairs.

(2) In the exercise of the powers conferred by this section regard shall be had first of all to the requirements of the patient, and the rules of law which restricted the enforcement by a creditor of rights against property under the control of the judge in lunacy shall apply

to property under the control of the judge; but, subject to the foregoing provisions of this subsection, the judge shall, in administering a patient's affairs, have regard to the interests of creditors and also to the desirability of making provision for obligations of the patient notwithstanding that they may not be legally enforceable.

96 Powers of the judge as to patient's property and affairs

(1) Without prejudice to the generality of section 95 above, the judge shall have power to make such orders and give such directions and authorities as he thinks fit for the purposes of that section and in particular may for those purposes make orders or give directions or authorities for –

(e) the execution for the patient of a will making any provision (whether by way of disposing of property or exercising a power or otherwise) which could be made by a will executed by the patient if he were not mentally disordered; ...

(4) The power of the judge to make or give an order, direction or authority for the execution of a will for a patient –

(a) shall not be exercisable at any time when the patient is a minor, and

(b) shall not be exercised unless the judge has reason to believe that the patient is incapable of making a valid will for himself.

97 Supplementary provisions as to wills executed under s96

(1) Where under section 96(1) above the judge makes or gives an order, direction or authority requiring or authorising a person (in this section referred to as 'the authorised person') to execute a will for a patient, any will executed in pursuance of that order, direction or authority shall be expressed to be signed by the patient acting by the authorised person, and shall be –

(a) signed by the authorised person with the name of the patient, and with his own name, in the presence of two or more witnesses present at the same time, and

(b) attested and subscribed by those witnesses in the presence of the authorised person, and

(c) sealed with the official seal of the Court of Protection.

(2) The Wills Act 1837 shall have effect in relation to any such will as if it were signed by the patient by his own hand, except that in relation to any such will –

(a) section 9 of that Act (which makes provision as to the signing and attestation of wills) shall not apply, and

(b) in the subsequent provisions of that Act any reference to execution in the manner required by the previous provisions of that Act shall be construed as a reference to execution in the manner required by subsection (1) above.

(3) Subject to the following provisions of this section, any such will executed in accordance with subsection (1) above shall have the same effect for all purposes as if the patient were capable of making a valid will and the will had been executed by him in the manner required by the Wills Act 1837.

(4) So much of subsection (3) above as provides for such a will to have effect as if the patient were capable of making a valid will –

(a) shall not have effect in relation to such a will in so far as it disposes of any immovable property, other than immovable property in England and Wales, and

(b) where at the time when such a will is executed the patient is domiciled in Scotland or Northern Ireland or in a country or territory outside the United Kingdom, shall not have effect in relation to that will in so far as it relates to any other property or matter, except any property or matter in respect of which, under the law of his domicile, any question of his testamentary capacity would fall to be determined in accordance with the law of England and Wales.

98   Judge's powers in cases of emergency

Where it is represented to the judge, and he has reason to believe, that a person may be incapable, by reason of mental disorder, of managing and administering his property and affairs, and the judge is of the opinion that it is necessary to make immediate provision for any of the matters referred to in section 95 above, then pending the determination of the question whether that person is so incapable the judge may exercise in relation to the property and affairs of that person any of the powers conferred on him in relation to the property and affairs of a patient by this Part of this Act so far as is requisite for enabling that provision to be made.

COUNTY COURTS ACT 1984
(1984 c 28)

23 Equity jurisdiction

A county court shall have all the jurisdiction of the High Court to hear and determine –

(a) proceedings for the administration of the estate of a deceased person, where the estate does not exceed in amount or value the county court limit;

(b) proceedings –

(i) for the execution of any trust, or

(ii) for a declaration that a trust subsists, or

(iii) under section 1 of the Variation of Trusts Act 1958,

where the estate or fund subject, or alleged to be subject, to the trust does not exceed in amount or value the county court limit; ...

(g) proceedings for relief against fraud or mistake, where the damage sustained or the estate or fund in respect of which relief is sought does not exceed in amount or value the county court limit.

24 Jurisdiction by agreement in certain equity proceedings

(1) If, as respects any proceedings to which this section applies, the parties agree, by a memorandum signed by them or by their respective legal representatives or agents, that a county court specified in the memorandum shall have jurisdiction in the proceedings, that court shall, notwithstanding anything in any enactment, have jurisdiction to hear and determine the proceedings accordingly.

(2) Subject to subsection (3), this section applies to any proceedings in which a county court would have jurisdiction by virtue of – ...

(d) sections 17(2), 38(4), 41(1A), and 43(4) of the Administration of Estates Act 1925, ...

(g) sections 23 and 25 of this Act,

but for the limits of the jurisdiction of the court provided in those enactments.

(3) This section does not apply to proceedings under section 1 of the Variation of Trusts Acts 1958.

25 Jurisdiction under Inheritance (Provision for Family and Dependants) Act 1975

A county court shall have jurisdiction to hear and determine any application for an order under section 2 of the Inheritance (Provision for Family and Dependants) Act 1975 (including any application for permission to apply for such an order and any application made, in the proceedings on an application for such an order, for an order under any other provision of that Act).

32 Contentious probate jurisdiction

(1) Where –

(a) an application for the grant or revocation of probate or administration has been made through the principal registry of the Family Division or district probate registry under section 105 of the Supreme Court Act 1981; and

(b) it is shown to the satisfaction of a county court that the value at the date of the death of the deceased of his net estate does not exceed the county court limit,

the county court shall have the jurisdiction of the High Court in respect of any contentious matter arising with the grant or revocation.

(2) In subsection (1) 'net estate', in relation to a deceased person, means the estate of that person exclusive of any property he was possessed of or entitled to as a trustee and not beneficially, and after making allowances for funeral expenses and for debts and liabilities.

Note. By virtue of the County Court Jurisdiction Order 1981, for the purposes of s23, above, the county court limit is £30,000.

As amended by the Administration of Justice Act 1985, s51(1); Courts and Legal Services Act 1990, s125(3), Schedule 18, para 49(3).

ADMINISTRATION OF JUSTICE ACT 1985

(1985 c 61)

48 Power of High Court to authorise action to be taken in reliance on counsel's opinion

(1) Where –

(a) any question of construction has arisen out of the terms of a will or a trust; and

(b) an opinion in writing given by a person who has a ten year High Court qualification, within the meaning of section 71 of the Courts and Legal Services Act 1990, has been obtained on that question by the personal representatives or trustees under the will or trust,

the High Court may, on the application of the personal representatives or trustees and without hearing argument, make an order authorising those persons to take such steps in reliance on the said opinion as are specified in the order.

(2) The High Court shall not make an order under subsection (1) if it appears to the court that a dispute exists which would make it inappropriate for the court to make the order without hearing argument.

49 Powers of High Court on compromise of probate action

(1) Where on a compromise of a probate action in the High Court –

(a) the court is invited to pronounce for the validity of one or more wills, or against the validity of one or more wills, or for the validity of one or more wills and against the validity of one or more other wills; and

(b) the court is satisfied that consent to the making of the pronouncement or, as the case may be, each of the pronouncements in question has been given by or on behalf of every relevant beneficiary,

the court may without more pronounce accordingly.

(2) In this section –

'probate action' means an action for the grant of probate of the will, or letters of administration of the estate, of a deceased person or for the revocation of such a grant or for a decree pronouncing for or against the validity of an alleged will, not being an action which is non-contentious or common form probate business; and

'relevant beneficiary', in relation to a pronouncement relating to any will or wills of a deceased person, means –

(a) a person who under any such will is beneficially interested in the deceased's estate; and

(b) where the effect of the pronouncement would be to cause the estate to devolve as on an intestacy (or partial intestacy), or to prevent it from so devolving, a person who under the law relating to intestacy is beneficially interested in the estate.

50 Power of High Court to appoint substitute for, or to remove, personal representative

(1) Where an application relating to the estate of a deceased person is made to the High Court under this subsection by or on behalf of a personal representative of the deceased or a beneficiary of the estate, the court may in its discretion –

(a) appoint a person (in this section called a substituted personal representative) to act as personal representative of the deceased in place of the existing personal representative or representatives of the deceased or any of them; or

(b) if there are two or more existing personal representatives of the deceased, terminate the appointment of one or more, but not all, of those persons.

(2) Where the court appoints a person to act as a substituted personal representative of a deceased person, then –

(a) if that person is appointed to act with an executor or executors the appointment shall (except for the purposes of including him in any chain of representation) constitute him executor of the deceased as from the date of the appointment; and

(b) in any other case the appointment shall constitute that person administrator of the deceased's estate as from the date of the appointment.

(3) The court may authorise a person appointed as a substituted personal representative to charge remuneration for his services as such, on such terms (whether or not involving the submission of bills of charges for taxation by the court) as the court may think fit.

(4) Where an applicant relating to the estate of a deceased person is made to the court under subsection (1), the court may, if it thinks fit, proceed as if the application were, or included, an application for the appointment under the Judicial Trustees Act 1896 of a judicial trustee in relation to that estate.

(5) In this section 'beneficiary', in relation to the estate of a deceased person, means a person who under the will of the deceased or under the law relating to intestacy is beneficially interested in the estate.

As amended by the Courts and Legal Services Act 1990, s71(2), Schedule 10, para 63.

FAMILY LAW REFORM ACT 1987
(1987 c 42)

1   General principle

(1) In this Act and enactments passed and instruments made after the coming into force of this section, references (however expressed) to any relationship between two persons shall, unless the contrary intention appears, be construed without regard to whether or not the father and mother of either of them, or the father and mother of any person through whom the relationship is deduced, have or had been married to each other at any time.

(2) In this Act and enactments passed after the coming into force of this section, unless the contrary intention appears –

(a) references to a person whose father and mother were married to each other at the time of his birth include; and

(b) references to a person whose father and mother were not married to each other at the time of his birth do not include,

references to any person to whom subsection (3) below applies, and cognate references shall be construed accordingly.

(3) This subsection applies to any person who –

(a) is treated as legitimate by virtue of section 1 of the Legitimacy Act 1976;

(b) is a legitimated person within the meaning of section 10 of that Act;

(c) is an adopted child within the meaning of Part IV of the Adoption Act 1976; or

(d) is otherwise treated in law as legitimate.

(4) For the purpose of construing references falling within subsection (2) above, the time of a person's birth shall be taken to include any time during the period beginning with –

(a) the insemination resulting in his birth; or

(b) where there was no such insemination, his conception,

and (in either case) ending with his birth.

18   Succession on intestacy

(1) In Part IV of the Administration of Estates Act 1925 (which deals with the distribution of the estate of an intestate), references (however expressed) to any relationship between two persons shall be construed in accordance with section 1 above.

(2) For the purposes of subsection (1) above and that Part of that Act, a person whose father and mother were not married to each other at the time of his birth shall be presumed not to have been survived by his father, or by any person related to him only through his father, unless the contrary is shown.

(3) In section 50(1) of that Act (which relates to the construction of documents), the reference to Part IV of that Act, or to the foregoing provisions of that Part, shall in relation to an instrument inter vivos made, or a will or codicil coming into operation, after the coming into force of this section (but not in relation to instruments inter vivos made or wills or codicils coming into operation earlier) be construed as including references to this section.

(4) This section does not affect any rights under the intestacy of a person dying before the coming into force of this section.

19   Dispositions of property

(1) In the following dispositions, namely –

   (a) dispositions inter vivos made on or after the date on which this section comes into force; and

   (b) dispositions by will or codicil where the will or codicil is made on or after that date,

references (whether express or implied) to any relationship between two persons shall be construed in accordance with section 1 above.

(2) It is hereby declared that the use, without more, of the word 'heir' or 'heirs' or any expression which is used to create an entailed interest in real or personal property does not show a contrary intention for the purposes of section 1 as applied by subsection (1) above.

(3) In relation to the dispositions mentioned in subsection (1) above, section 33 of the Trustee Act 1925 (which specifies the trust implied by a direction that income is to be held on protective trusts for the benefit of any person) shall have effect as if any reference (however expressed) to any relationship between two persons were construed in accordance with section 1 above.

(4) Where under any disposition of real or personal property, any interest in such property is limited (whether subject to any preceding limitation or charge or not) in such a way that it would, apart from this section, devolve (as nearly as the law permits) along with a dignity or title of honour, then –

(a) whether or not the disposition contains an express reference to the dignity or title of honour; and

(b) whether or not the property or some interest in the property may in some event become severed from it,

nothing in this section shall operate to sever the property or any interest in it from the dignity or title, but the property or interest shall devolve in all respects as if this section had not been enacted.

(5) This section is without prejudice to section 42 of the Adoption Act 1976 (construction of dispositions in cases of adoption).

(6) In this section 'disposition' means a disposition, including an oral disposition, of real or personal property whether inter vivos or by will or codicil.

(7) Notwithstanding any rule of law, a disposition made by will or codicil executed before the date on which this section comes into force shall not be treated for the purposes of this section as made on or after that date by reason only that the will or codicil is confirmed by a codicil executed on or after that date.

21 Entitlement to grant of probate, etc

(1) For the purpose of determining the person or persons who would in accordance with probate rules be entitled to a grant of probate or administration in respect of the estate of a deceased person, the deceased shall be presumed, unless the contrary is shown, not to have been survived –

(a) by any person related to him whose father and mother were not married to each other at the time of his birth; or

(b) by any person whose relationship with him is deduced through such a person as is mentioned in paragraph (a) above.

(2) In this section 'probate rules' means rules of court made under section 127 of the Supreme Court Act 1981.

(3) This section does not apply in relation to the estate of a person dying before the coming into force of this section.

COPYRIGHT, DESIGNS AND PATENTS ACT 1988
(1988 c 48)

90   Assignment and licences

(1) Copyright is transmissible by assignment, by testamentary disposition or by operation of law, as personal or moveable property.

(2) An assignment or other transmission of copyright may be partial, that is, limited so as to apply –

(a) to one or more, but not all, of the things the copyright owner has the exclusive right to do;

(b) to part, but not the whole, of the period for which the copyright is to subsist ...

93   Copyright to pass under will with unpublished work

Where under a bequest (whether specific or general) a person is entitled, beneficially or otherwise, to –

(a) an original document or other material thing recording or embodying a literary, dramatic, musical or artistic work which was not published before the death of the testator, or

(b) an original material thing containing a sound recording or film which was not published before the death of the testator,

the bequest shall, unless a contrary intention is indicated in the testator's will or a codicil to it, be construed as including the copyright in the work in so far as the testator was the owner of the copyright immediately before his death.

CHILDREN ACT 1989
(1989 c 41)

5   Appointment of guardians

(3) A parent who has parental responsibility for his child may appoint another individual to be the child's guardian in the event of his death.

(4) A guardian of a child may appoint another individual to take his place as the child's guardian in the event of his death.

(5) An appointment under subsection (3) or (4) shall not have effect unless it is made in writing, is dated and is signed by the person making the appointment or –

(a) in the case of an appointment made by a will which is not signed by the testator, is signed at the direction of the testator in accordance with the requirements of section 9 of the Wills Act 1837; or

(b) in any other case, is signed at the direction of the person making the appointment, in his presence and in the presence of two witnesses who each attest the signature.

(6) A person appointed as a child's guardian under this section shall have parental responsibility for the child concerned ...

(10) Nothing in this section shall be taken to prevent an appointment under subsection (3) or (4) being made by two or more persons acting jointly ...

6   Guardians: revocation and disclaimer

(1) An appointment under section 5(3) or (4) revokes an earlier such appointment (including one made in an unrevoked will or codicil) made by the same person in respect of the same child, unless it is clear (whether as the result of an express provision in the later appointment or by any necessary implication) that the purpose of the later appointment is to appoint an additional guardian.

(2) An appointment under section 5(3) or (4) (including one made in an unrevoked will or codicil) is revoked if the person who made the appointment revokes it by a written and dated instrument which is signed –

(a) by him; or

(b) at his direction, in his presence and in the presence of two witnesses who each attest the signature ...

(4) For the avoidance of doubt, an appointment under section 5(3) or (4) made in a will or codicil is revoked if the will or codicil is revoked.

(5) A person who is appointed as a guardian under section 5(3) or (4) may disclaim his appointment by an instrument in writing signed by him and made within a reasonable time of his first knowing that the appointment has taken effect ...

(7) Any appointment of a guardian under section 5 may be brought to an end at any time by order of the court –

(a) on the application of any person who has parental responsibility for the child;

(b) on the application of the child concerned, with leave of the court; or

(c) in any family proceedings, if the court considers that it should be brought to an end even though no application has been made.